2019 Microsoft Excel®
For Beginners

+

30 Formulas & Features
The Step-By-Step Guide

C.J. Benton

ISBN: 9781674846804

Thank you!

Thank you for purchasing and reading this book! **Your feedback is valued and appreciated.** Please take a few minutes and leave a review.

More books by this author:

For a complete list please visit us at:
https://bentonbooks.wixsite.com/bentonbooks/buy-books

- **Excel 2019** Pivot Tables & Introduction To Dashboards The Step-By-Step Guide
- Excel Pivot Tables & Introduction To Dashboards The Step-By-Step Guide *(version 2016)*
- **Excel 2019** VLOOKUP The Step-By-Step Guide
- Excel Macros & VBA For Business Users - A Beginners Guide

Questions, comments?
Please contact us at:

Email: bentontrainingbooks@gmail.com
Website: https://bentonbooks.wixsite.com/bentonbooks

CHAPTER 1

Microsoft® Excel® is a spreadsheet program allowing users to organize, report, calculate, track, and perform analysis on virtually any type of data. It is part of the Microsoft® Office® suite. At time of this publication, the collection of software products is available in three forms:

1) **Office v2019**, along with earlier versions[1] require the software to be installed onto a laptop or desktop computer. You pay a one-time fee and receive a license for three to seven of the below applications.

2) **Office 365** is a subscription based model, where you pay a monthly or annual fee to use the suite. Office 365 provides full access to the seven products listed below. Office 365 has no versions, with the subscription you always have the most up-to-date edition.

3) **Office Online** is a free, scaled down version (limited feature set) of Office 365, however it does not include **Publisher®** or **Access®**.

Pricing[2] for Office v2019 or Office 365 varies depending on home or business use. Microsoft® does offer discounts to select educators, students, and non-profits.

1. **Access®** *(a database application)*
2. **Excel®** *(please see definition below)*
3. **OneNote®** *(stores text, web links, images and other information)*
4. **Outlook®** *(an email application)*
5. **PowerPoint®** *(a presentation / slideshow program)*
6. **Publisher®** *(create professional looking flyers, brochures, etc.)*
7. **Word®** *(a word processing application)*

---

[1] *Previous versions of Microsoft® Office®, retrieved 9 December 2019*
https://products.office.com/en-us/previous-versions-of-office

[2] *Microsoft® Office® pricing, retrieved 9 December 2019*
https://products.office.com/en-us/compare-all-microsoft-office-products?&activetab=tab:primaryr1

The four most widely used applications of the suite are, **Word®**, **Outlook®**, **PowerPoint®**, and **Excel®**.

> Excel® is a spreadsheet program allowing users to organize, report, calculate, track, and perform analysis on virtually any type of data.

With Excel®, users can create everything from simple lists and perform basic arithmetic calculations to interfacing with external databases and analyzing millions of records. Sophisticated engineering calculations and statistics can be completed in milliseconds. Repetitive spreadsheet tasks can be automated and performed with a single click of a button.

Formatting, graphs, and other presentation tools allow you to easily create professionally looking budgets, reports, estimates, invoices, lists, charts, matrices, virtually any type of artifact containing text, currency, numeric, or time values.

Excel® is also the application that interfaces the most with other software programs in the Microsoft® Office® suite. For example, if you had customer and sales information contained in Excel® you could export these records into Word® and create client invoices.

You may easily import data from Access® or a multitude of other data sources for analysis, testing, project schedules, and more.

There are hundreds of templates and pre-made spreadsheets available for download³. These can save you time or serve as inspiration for designing your own worksheets.

Excel® is perhaps the most versatile and flexible application ever developed. Basic knowledge and experience with Excel®, along with Word® and Outlook®, are required skills for many professions and college students.

---

³*Featured Templates for Excel® provided by Microsoft®, retrieved 9 December 2019*
https://templates.office.com/en-us/templates-for-Excel#

In the following, pages we'll introduce you to the basic functionality of Excel®. We'll review the most commonly used toolbar (Ribbon) commands, how to create a new spreadsheet, including formatting, saving, and printing. In addition to this, you'll learn how to apply 30 of the most frequently used formulas and features, including a step-by-step example creating a basic Pivot Table.

When finished, you'll have a solid understanding of Excel® and be ready to take the next step in your education of the Microsoft® Office® suite.

TRAINING SEGMENTS

This book is divided into three sections and may be used as a tutorial or quick reference guide. It is intended for those who are new to Excel® or for those who would like to improve their Excel® skills.

All of the examples in this book use **Microsoft Excel® 2019**, however most of the functionality may be applied using Microsoft Excel® version 2016. **All screenshots in this book use Microsoft Excel® 2019.** There are no examples or review using Office 365 or Office Online.

While this book provides a general overview and several examples, it does not cover all available Microsoft Excel® features, formulas, and functionality.

Please always **back-up your work** and **save often**. A good best practice when attempting any new work is to **create a copy of the original spreadsheet** and implement your changes on the copied spreadsheet. Should anything go wrong, you then have the original spreadsheet to refer back to. Please see the diagram below.

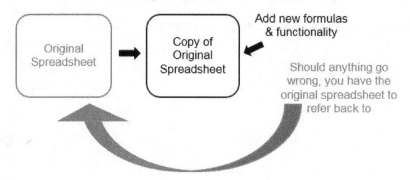

LIST OF FORMULAS & FEATURES DETAILED IN THIS BOOK

Step-By-Step examples for the following formulas and features:

FORMULAS	FEATURES
1. Average	26. AutoFilters
2. AverageIF	27. Charts
3. Concat	28. Conditional Formatting
4. CountIF	29. Data Sorting
5. CountIFs	30. Pivot Tables
6. Division	
7. IF	***Plus:***
8. IFError	• Creating A New Spreadsheet
9. Len	• Saving Files
10. Lower	• Printing Spreadsheets
11. Max	
12. Mid	
13. Min	
14. Multiplication	
15. NetWorkDays	
16. Proper	
17. Round	
18. Subtraction	
19. Sum *(addition)*	
20. SumIF	
21. Text	
22. Today & Now	
23. Trim	
24. Upper	
25. Vlookup	

FILES FOR EXERCISES

The exercise files are available for download at the following website:
https://bentonbooks.wixsite.com/bentonbooks/excel-2019

All files are saved in **Excel® version 2019**

SECTION ~ ONE

- BASIC COMMANDS

To begin, we'll first review how to open Excel® and create a blank spreadsheet.

STARTING EXCEL®

To open Excel®:
1. Click the **'Start'** (Windows) button and scroll to the letter **'E'**
2. Select the program **'Excel'***

*This method is for Excel® **version 2019**, earlier versions would be accessed differently.*

Alternatively:

▪ From the taskbar, select the Excel® icon:

Click the Excel icon from your taskbar

CREATING A NEW SPREADSHEET (STEP-BY-STEP EXAMPLE)

Once Excel® has opened, your screen will look *similar* to the following:

You'll notice pre-made templates available. The best practice is to first learn the basic functionality of Excel® before using these. Once you have a better understanding of Excel®, you may modify and verify the calculations in these templates meet your requirements.

1. Select the 'Blank Workbook' option

After you click the **'Blank Workbook'** option, you will have created a **'workbook'** file, made up of one or more worksheets.

Entire screen is not displayed for easier viewing:

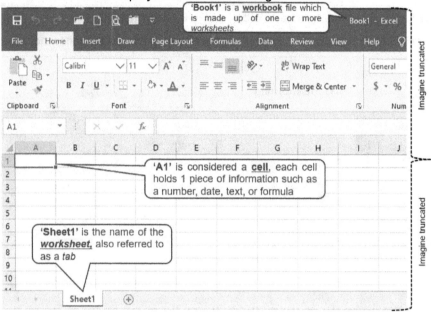

WORKBOOK

> A **workbook** file is made up of one or more worksheets. Worksheets are also referred to as tabs.

WORKSHEET

> A **worksheet** is made of up cells displayed in a grid of rows and columns

---

CELL

> A **cell** holds one piece of information such as a number, currency value, date, text, or formula.

Next, let's review how to navigate and customize the toolbar (Ribbon) and Quick Access Toolbar.

TOOLBAR (RIBBON)

The **toolbar** or what Microsoft® calls the **'Ribbon'** consists of *tabs* that contain *commands*. There are ten default tabs.

1. File	6. Formulas
2. Home	7. Data
3. Insert	8. Review
4. Draw	9. View
5. Page Layout	10. Help

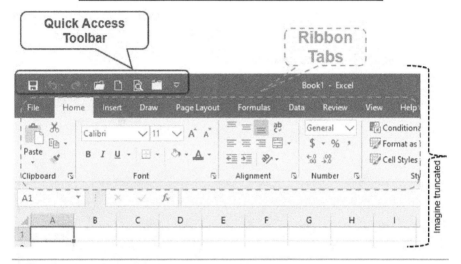

QUICK ACCESS TOOLBAR

The **Quick Access Toolbar** sets on top of the **Ribbon.** Think of this as a place to add procedures you use the most often. For example, buttons to *save*, *print*, *undo*, or *create a new workbook* file. These commands stay constant, regardless of what Ribbon tab is active.

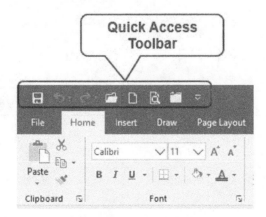

CUSTOMIZING THE RIBBON & QUICK ACCESS TOOLBAR

Both the **Quick Access Toolbar** and the **Ribbon** are customizable. I find it more efficient to modify the Quick Access Toolbar. However, you may prefer to change the Ribbon.

Below are the steps to remove or add buttons to both the Quick Access Toolbar and Ribbon.

To **add** a command button:

1. Click drop-down arrow on the **'Quick Access Toolbar'**
2. Select **'More Commands...'**

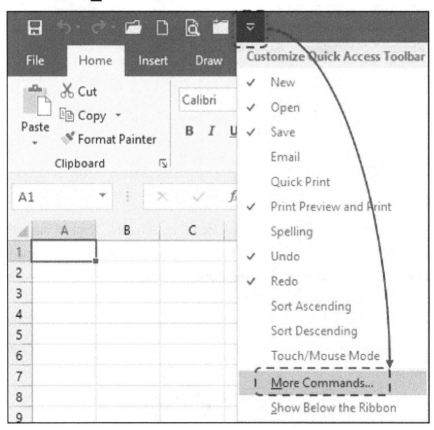

Alternatively, you may **right-click** over the **'Ribbon'** or the **'Quick Access Toolbar** to receive the below prompt:

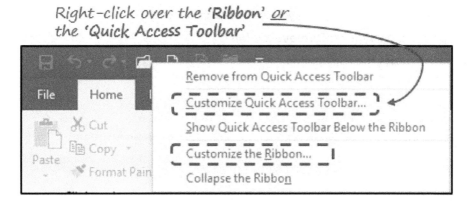

The following prompt will appear:

3. Select either **'Quick Access Toolbar'** _or_ **'Customize Ribbon'**

4. Select a command you would like to add

5. Select the **'Add>>'** button

6. Click the **'OK'** button

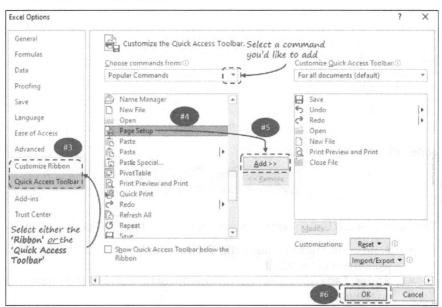

To **remove** a command button:

1. Click drop-down arrow on the **'Quick Access Toolbar'**

2. Select **'More Commands...'**

3. Select either **'Quick Access Toolbar'** _or_ **'Customize Ribbon'**

4. Select a command you would like to remove

5. Select the **'<<Remove'** button

6. Click the **'OK'** button

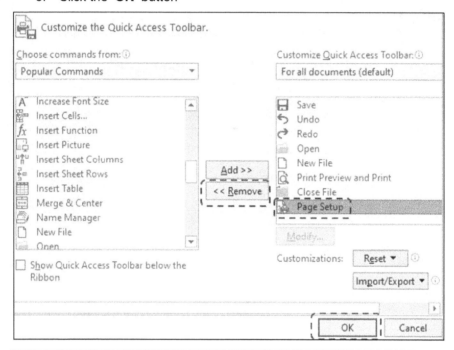

RIBBON & WORKBOOK DISPLAY OPTIONS

Across from the Quick Access Toolbar in the top left corner you'll notice a series of small icons.

The ⬆️ up arrow button, when clicked, will present three Ribbon options:

- **Auto-hide Ribbon** hides the Ribbon, until you click the top of a worksheet to unhide it
- **Show Tabs** displays the tab name only, but not the individual commands
- **Show Tabs and Commands** displays both the tab name and the commands *(this is the default setting)*

The ▬ underscore button when clicked, will **minimize** the active workbook

The ⧉ double window button when clicked, will **resize** the active workbook

The ✕ cross (X) button when clicked, will **close** the active workbook (*you'll be prompted to save your file if you've not already done so*)

Lastly, let's take a quick look at a few more parts of the worksheet before we delve into the specifics of the Ribbon menu options.

NAME BOX

The **'Name Box'** indicates the location of the *active cell*

FORMULA BAR

The **'Formula Bar'** displays the **'syntax'** of a formula or displays a number, date, currency, or text value of the *active cell*.

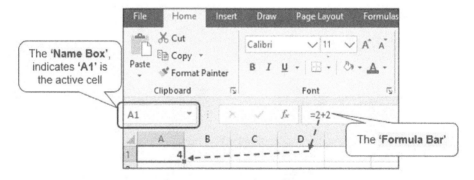

Syntax

Syntax in Excel® refers to the arrangement or order of a formula or function. All formulas & functions begin with the equal sign (=) followed by numbers or the function's name.

We'll further review the meaning of syntax in *chapter 4* **'Basic Formulas'** *Sum, Subtraction, Multiplication, & Division'*

SECTION ~ TWO

- *TOOLBAR (RIBBON)*
NAVIGATION

As we review the Ribbon menus, you'll find Excel® offers multiple ways to accomplish the same functionality. For example, you may *print* a worksheet by:

1. Selecting from the Ribbon **File : Print** and clicking the '**Print**' button

2. Selecting from the Ribbon **Page Layout**, expanding the '**Page Setup**' submenu and clicking the '**Print**' button

3. Clicking the '**Print Preview and Print**' icon from the '**Quick Access Toolbar**' and clicking the '**Print**' button

4. From your keyboard, pressing shortcut keys **(CTRL + P)** and clicking the '**Print**' button

No method is better, it's simply a matter of personal preference.

Next, we'll review 8 out of the 10 Ribbon menus. The overview will cover the main functionality of eight menus, however not all available commands are discussed. The '**Draw**' & '**Page Layout**' menus are not evaluated as either the functionality is covered in other sections of the book or is infrequently used.

FILE

The '**FILE**' tab contains commands for saving, printing, and changing the Excel® application settings.

SAVING FILES (STEP-BY STEP EXAMPLE)

To **save** a workbook file:

1. Open the Excel® application and click the '**Blank workbook**' icon

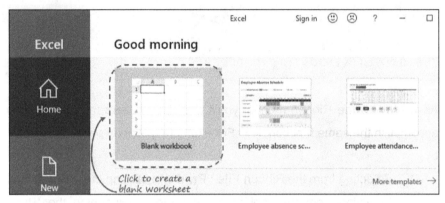

2. Enter the text **test** into cell **'A1'**

3. Click the **'File'** tab

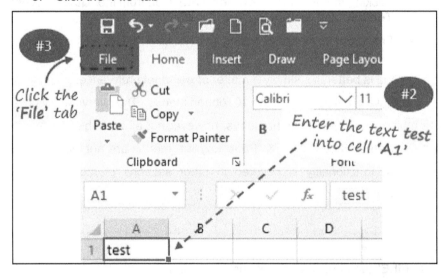

4. Click **'Save As'**

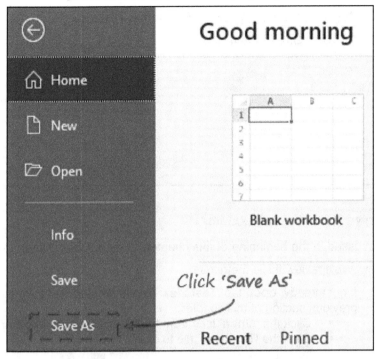

5. Click the **'Browse'** option to select a *location* on your computer to save the file

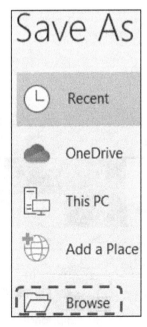

6. When prompted, provide the **File name: Test.xlsx**

7. Click the **'Save'** button

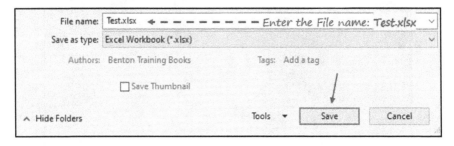

PRINTING (STEP-BY-STEP EXAMPLE)

As discussed in the beginning of this chapter, there are four different ways to print. We'll review three methods:

1. If not already, **open** the **'Test.xlsx'** file we created and saved in the previous section of this chapter:
   - Click the **'Open'** icon from the **'Quick Access Toolbar'**
   - Click the **'Test.xlsx'** file to open

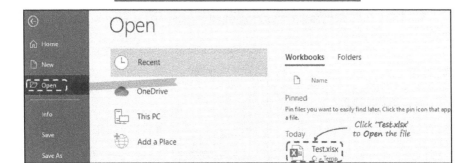

2. Click the **'File'** tab

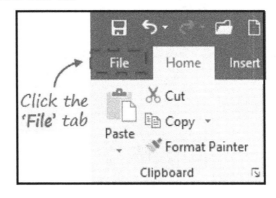

3. Click **'Print'**

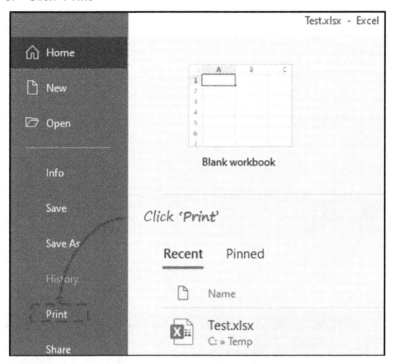

Alternatively:

- Click the **'Print Preview and Print'** icon from the **'Quick Access Toolbar'**, once added to your 'Quick Access Toolbar' *(please see chapter 2 for instructions on how to add commands to the Quick Access Toolbar)*

Using either approach will launch the following prompt

4. Click the **'Print'** button *(the workbook would print assuming you have correctly installed a printer)*

ADDITIONAL PRINT SETTINGS (THE PAGE LAYOUT TAB)

The worksheets we develop typically appear nicely formatted in electronic form, however if a user prints the spreadsheet often times the information is truncated and the report prints unnecessarily in multiple pages.

For example, the information contained in the below report is cutoff in multiple sections and prints out in 3 pages. A reader would have a difficult time understanding the content or be inconvenienced by having to adjust the print settings themselves.

The right section of the spreadsheet is truncated

REGIONS		SALES BY CATEGORY		Employe 5% c

REGIONS	SALES_$	CATEGORY	SALES_$	EMPLOYEE
Central	$7,271	Electrical	$11,641	Simpson, Helen
East	$6,931	Interior	$3,499	Perry, Chloe
North	$7,859	Other	$7,013	Long, Elenor
South	$7,596	Power Train	$9,262	Becker, Sam
West	$7,503	Structural	$5,745	Russell, Penelo
TOTAL	$37,160	TOTAL	$37,160	Bennett, Lucy
				Williams, Jasmi

% of Sales by Category

Structural
16%

Electrical
31%

Missing the lower half of the chart

The following *is not* a step-by-step example, instead demonstrates through screenshots how to:

- Change the **'Orientation'** from **'Portrait'** to **'Landscape'**
- Adjust the margin settings
- Add a **Header or Footer** (page numbers)

The presentation uses the **Page Layout** menu from the Ribbon:

A. Expand the **'Page Setup'** section by clicking the diagonal arrow

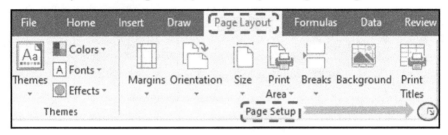

The following dialogue box will appear:

B. Select the **'Landscape'** radio button
C. Change the **'Scaling'** by selecting the **'Fit to'** radio button *(this will ensure the report prints on 1 page)*
D. Select the **'Margins'** tab

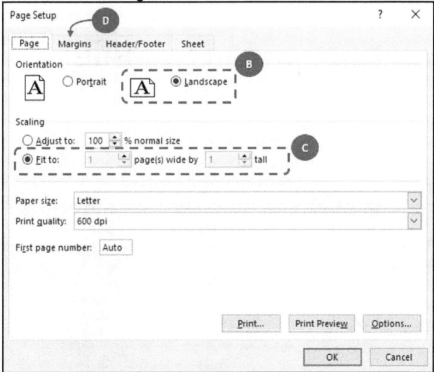

E. Select the '**Center on page : Horizontally'** check box

F. Select the **'Header/Footer'** tab

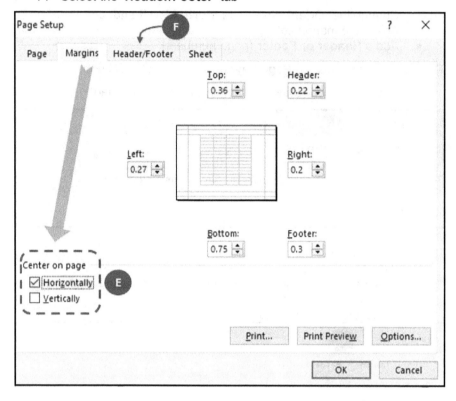

G. Select the button **'Custom Header…'** the title **'Monthly Dashboard'** was added

H. Select a drop-down list for **'Footer:'** by selecting **'Page 1 of ?'**. The **'?'** will automatically populate to the number of pages selected for printing, i.e. Page 1 of **3**

I. Click the **'Print Preview'** button

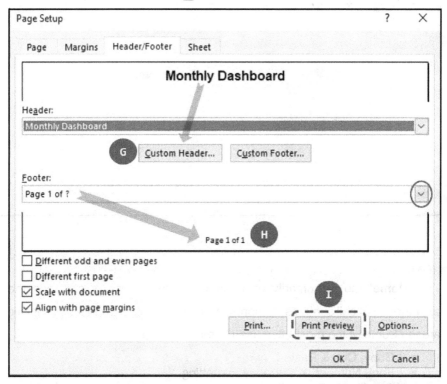

We may now click the **'Print'** button and print our report as a single page.

Example of a print friendly spreadsheet with a **Header & Footer** added:

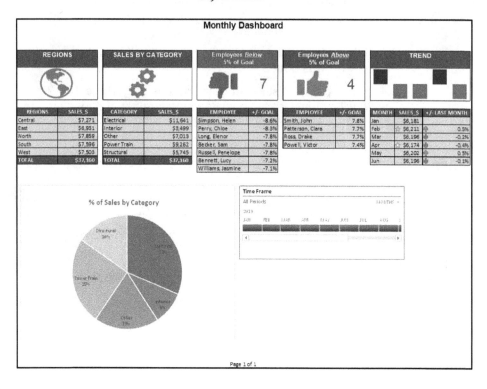

HOME

The **'Home'** tab is primarily used for formatting, which is changing the appearance of cell contents to improve readability or to draw focus to specific areas. Some of the most often used commands are:

- Copy, Cut, & Paste
- Font, Number, & Currency formatting
- Conditional Formatting

Toolbar is split for easier viewing:

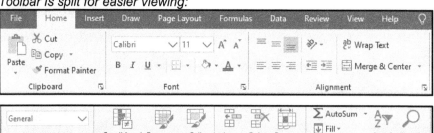

COPY

To **copy** the contents of one more cells:

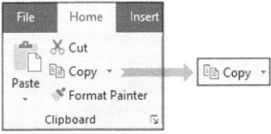

Select the cells you wish to copy and choose one of the following options:

- From the **Ribbon : Home** (tab), click the **'Copy'** button *(please see above screenshot)*

- Clicking the **'Copy'** icon from the **'Quick Access Toolbar'** - *once added to your 'Quick Access Toolbar' (please see chapter 2 for instructions on how to add commands to the Quick Access Toolbar)*

- From your keyboard press shortcut keys (**CTRL+C**)

- Right-clicking over the cell(s) to be copied and selecting **'Copy'**

CUT

To **cut**, remove the contents of one more cells and move it to another location:

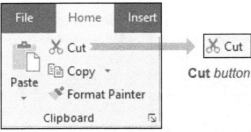

Cut *button*

Select the cells you wish to cut (move) and choose one of the following options:

- From the **Ribbon : Home** (tab), click the **'Cut'** button *(please see above screenshot)*

- Clicking the **'Cut'** icon from the **'Quick Access Toolbar'** - *once added to your 'Quick Access Toolbar' (please see chapter 2 for instructions on how to add commands to the Quick Access Toolbar)*

- From your keyboard press shortcut keys (**CTRL+X**)

- Right-clicking over the cell(s) to be cut and selecting '**Cut**'

PASTE

To **paste**, the contents of one more cells *after* they have been copied or cut to another location:

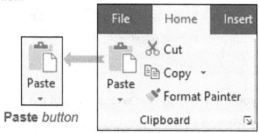

Select the cells you wish to paste (move) and choose one of the following options:

- From the **Ribbon : Home** (tab), click the '**Paste**' button *(please see above screenshot)*

- Clicking the '**Paste**' icon from the '**Quick Access Toolbar**' *- once added to your 'Quick Access Toolbar' (please see chapter 2 for instructions on how to add commands to the Quick Access Toolbar)*

- From your keyboard press shortcut keys (**CTRL+V**)

- Clicking the '**Paste**' **drop-down arrow** and selecting one of the '**Paste Special**' commands:

The *main* '**Paste Special**' options are:

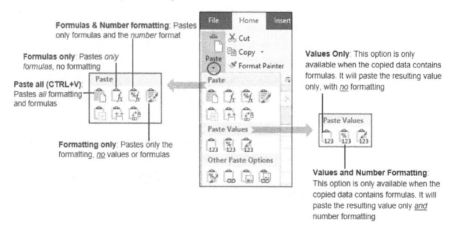

26

FONT OPTIONS

To change the font *style*, color, and size of the contents of cell, select one of the following options:

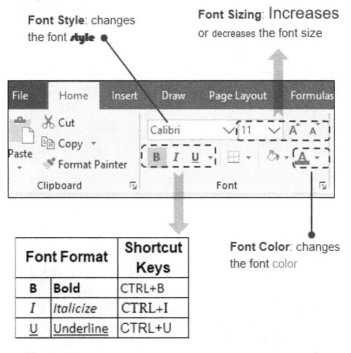

Font Style: changes the font *style*

Font Sizing: Increases or decreases the font size

Font Color: changes the font color

Font Format		Shortcut Keys
B	**Bold**	CTRL+B
I	*Italicize*	CTRL+I
U	Underline	CTRL+U

CELL - FORMATTING

To add cell shading and / or gridlines:

To add gridlines to a cell

To change the cell shading

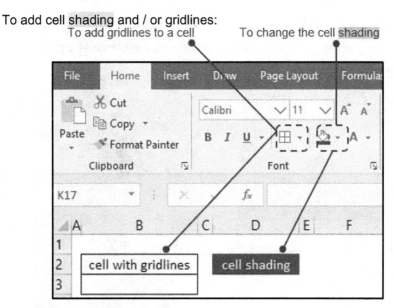

CURRENCY - FORMATTING

To change the format of a number to a currency.

Option 1: select the cells you want to apply a currency and from the **Ribbon : Home** (tab) click the **$** (symbol) button. Along with the adjoining commands to increase 100.**00** or decrease 100.**0** the number of decimal places.

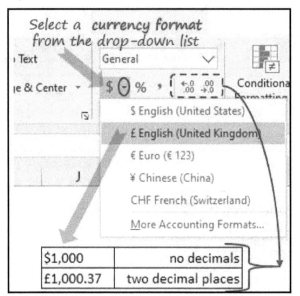

Option 2: if your currency is not listed in the **Ribbon : Home** (tab) **$** drop-down list, you may:

A. Select the cells you want to apply a currency

B. Expand the **'Number'** section by clicking the diagonal arrow

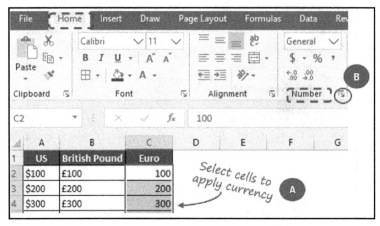

The following dialogue box will appear:

C. Select **'Currency'**

D. Click the drop-down arrow for **'Symbol:'**

E. Select your currency

F. Click the **'OK'** button

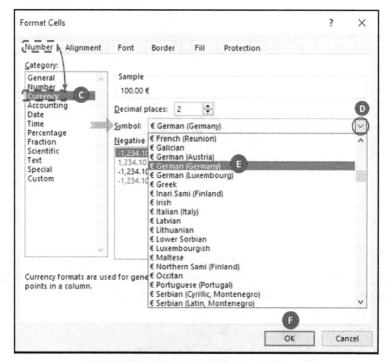

	A	B	C
1	**US**	**British Pound**	**Euro**
2	$100	£100	100.00 €
3	$200	£200	200.00 €
4	$300	£300	300.00 €
5	$400	£400	400.00 €
6	$500	£500	500.00 €

NUMBER & PERCENT - FORMATTING

The below buttons will change a value to a *percentage* **%** or back to a *number*

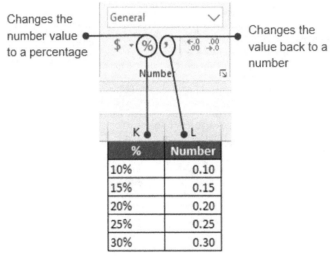

Changes the number value to a percentage

Changes the value back to a number

%	Number
10%	0.10
15%	0.15
20%	0.20
25%	0.25
30%	0.30

CONDITIONAL FORMATTING (STEP-BY-STEP EXAMPLE)

Using different colors for cell shading and fonts, Conditional Formatting allows you to highlight cells based on *specific criteria*.

✓ Preset options include:
  - The Top & Bottom 10 *(the number 10 can be adjusted)*
  - The Top & Bottom 10% *(the percentage can be adjusted)*
  - Above & Below the Average

✓ A very useful tool to quickly identify:
  - Duplicate values
  - A reoccurring date
  - Values greater or less than a specific number
  - Values equal to a specific number
  - Cells that contain specific text

WEB ADDRESS & FILE NAME FOR EXERCISE:

https://bentonbooks.wixsite.com/bentonbooks/excel-2019
MinAndMaxFormulas.xlsx

Scenario:

You've been given a spreadsheet that contains the total fruit sales by quarter and sales person. You've been asked to provide the *sales people* in which:
  - Sales are greater than $10,000
  - Sales are less than $1,000

Sample data, due to space limitations **the entire data set is not displayed**.

	A	B	C	D	E	F	G
1	SALES PERSON FIRST NAME	SALES PERSON LAST NAME	QUARTER	TOTAL		BEST SALES	WORST SALES
2	Jack	Smith	1	$ 343			
3	Jack	Smith	2	$ 1,849			
4	Jack	Smith	3	$ 2,653			
5	Jack	Smith	4	$ 5,494			
6	Joe	Tanner	1	$ 377			
7	Joe	Tanner	2	$ 2,404			
8	Joe	Tanner	3	$ 3,980			
9	Joe	Tanner	4	$ 39,631			
25	Billy	Winchester	4	$ 8,516			

1. Open the spreadsheet MinAndMaxFormulas.xlsx

2. Select **column 'D'**

3. From the Ribbon select **Home : Conditional Formatting**

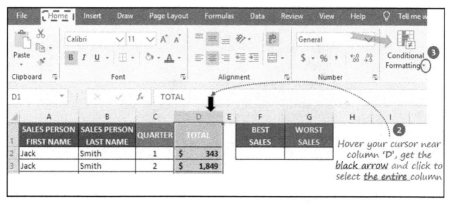

4. Select **Highlight Cells Rules > Greater Than…**

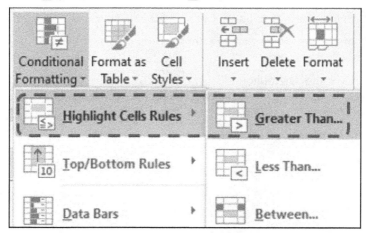

5. In the **'Format cells that are GREATER THAN':** box enter **10,000**

6. In the **'with'** box, click the drop-down arrow and select 'Green Fill with Dark Green Text'

7. Click the **'OK'** button

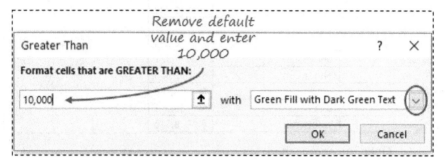

8. Repeat **steps 2 & 3** above

9. This time select <u>Highlight Cells Rules : Less Than…</u>

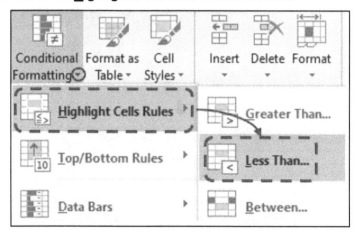

10. In the **'Format cells that are LESS THAN':** box enter **1,000**

11. In the **'with'** box click the drop-down arrow and select 'Light Red Fill with Dark Red Text'

12. Click the **'Ok'** button

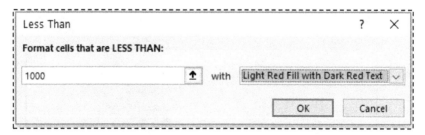

You've now provided a report displaying the *sales people* in which:
- Sales are greater than $10,000
- Sales are less than $1,000

*Due to space limitations **the entire report is not displayed**.*

	A	B	C	D
1	SALES PERSON FIRST NAME	SALES PERSON LAST NAME	QUARTER	TOTAL
2	Jack	Smith	1	$ 343
3	Jack	Smith	2	$ 1,849
4	Jack	Smith	3	$ 2,653
5	Jack	Smith	4	$ 5,494
6	Joe	Tanner	1	$ 377
7	Joe	Tanner	2	$ 2,404
8	Joe	Tanner	3	$ 3,980
9	Joe	Tanner	4	$ 39,631
10	Peter	Graham	1	$ 415
11	Peter	Graham	2	$ 3,125
12	Peter	Graham	3	$ 5,969
13	Peter	Graham	4	$ 13,199
14	Helen	Simpson	1	$ 457
15	Helen	Simpson	2	$ 4,062
16	Helen	Simpson	4	$ 8,954
17	Helen	Simpson	4	$ 20,459

Removing Conditional Formatting

To remove the Conditional Formatting:

1. From the Ribbon select **Home : Conditional Formatting:**

2. Select '**Clear Rules**' and *either* option:
   - Clear Rules from Select Cells
   - Clear Rules from Entire Sheet

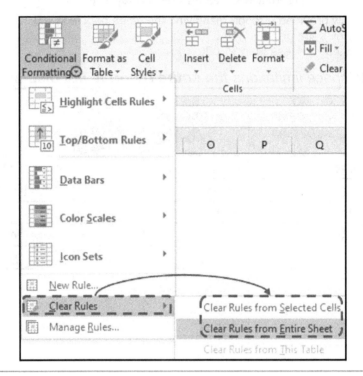

INSERT

The **'INSERT'** tab is comprised of two main areas:
1)   PivotTables &
2)   Presentation elements such as Charts, Illustrations, and Sparklines

Some of the most often used commands are:
- PivotTables
- Charts
- Sparklines
- Slicers & Timelines

Toolbar is split for easier viewing:

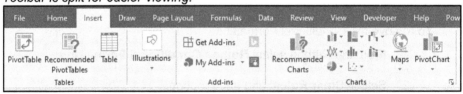

PIVOT TABLES

As your experience with Excel® grows, you'll likely start working with more and more data. PivotTables, allow you to quickly organize and summarize large amounts of information.

> **Pivot Tables** use built-in filters and functions to quickly organize, summarize, and filter large amounts of records.

PivotTables take individual cells or pieces of data and lets you arrange them into numerous types of calculated views. These snapshots of summarized data, require minimal effort to create and can be changed by simply clicking or dragging fields within your report.

By using built-in functions and filters, you may filter and drill-down for more detailed examination of your numbers. Various types of analysis can be completed without the need to manually enter formulas into the spreadsheet you're analyzing.

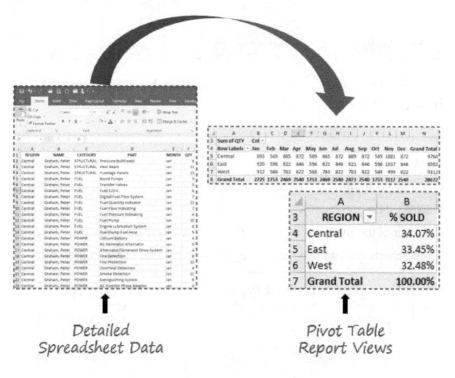

Detailed
Spreadsheet Data

Pivot Table
Report Views

For example, the below PivotTable is based on a detailed spreadsheet of 3,888 individual records containing information about airplane parts. In less than 1 minute, I was able to produce the following report for the quantity of parts sold by region:

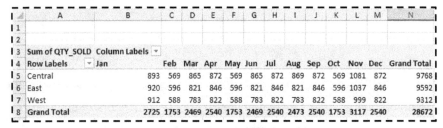

	A	B	C	D	E	F	G	H	I	J	K	L	M	N
1														
2														
3	Sum of QTY_SOLD	Column Labels ▾												
4	Row Labels ▾	Jan		Feb	Mar	Apr	May	Jun	Jul	Aug	Sep	Oct	Nov	Dec	Grand Total
5	Central		893	569	865	872	569	865	872	869	872	569	1081	872	9768
6	East		920	596	821	846	596	821	846	821	846	596	1037	846	9592
7	West		912	588	783	822	588	783	822	783	822	588	999	822	9312
8	Grand Total		2725	1753	2469	2540	1753	2469	2540	2473	2540	1753	3117	2540	28672

These PivotTable reports can also be formatted to improve readability. However, formatting does require a little more time to complete.

Formatted example:

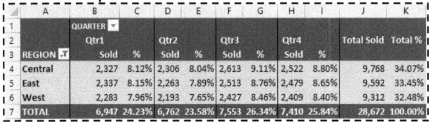

	A	B	C	D	E	F	G	H	I	J	K
1		QUARTER ▾									
2		Qtr1		Qtr2		Qtr3		Qtr4		Total Sold	Total %
3	REGION ▾	Sold	%	Sold	%	Sold	%	Sold	%		
4	Central	2,327	8.12%	2,306	8.04%	2,613	9.11%	2,522	8.80%	9,768	34.07%
5	East	2,337	8.15%	2,263	7.89%	2,513	8.76%	2,479	8.65%	9,592	33.45%
6	West	2,283	7.96%	2,193	7.65%	2,427	8.46%	2,409	8.40%	9,312	32.48%
7	TOTAL	6,947	24.23%	6,762	23.58%	7,553	26.34%	7,410	25.84%	28,672	100.00%

Please see chapter 14, for a **step-by-step example** on how to create a basic PivotTable.

CHARTS

Similarly, as with PivotTables, when you start working with more data, charting is another summarization tool. Only instead of using tables, it displays data graphically.

Four of the most common Chart types are; **Bar, Column, Pie** and **Line**. These charts fall into two main categories; 1) comparison and 2) trend.

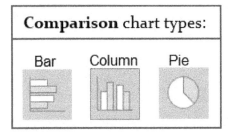

Comparison chart types:

Bar   Column   Pie

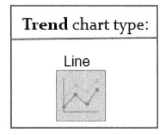

Trend chart type:

Line

Bar and **Column** charts are best for comparing numbers, such as currency or quantity. *Column* charts display data vertically, and are a better choice if your data includes <u>negative values</u>.

Pie charts also compare data and are ideal for illustrating percentages as part of the whole, like sales or product <u>allocation</u>.

Line charts are used to demonstrate <u>changes over a period of time</u> and are helpful in understanding trends. Often used when studying financial or frequency figures.

Let's walk through a Pie Chart example using Police Crime data.

WEB ADDRESS & FILE NAME FOR EXERCISE:
https://bentonbooks.wixsite.com/bentonbooks/excel-2019
PieChart.xlsx

PIE CHART (STEP-BY-STEP EXAMPLE)

<u>Scenario:</u>
Let's say you're an analyst and want to understand if crimes are occurring more often in a particular area of the county.

Sample data:

	A	B
1	AREA	COUNT OF CRIMES
2	EAST	810
3	NORTH	1,967
4	SOUTH	783
5	SOUTHWEST	560
6	WEST	1,654

1. Open the PieChart.xlsx spreadsheet
2. Select cells **'A1:B6'**
3. From the Ribbon select **Insert** and click the **PieChart** icon
4. Select the first **'2-D Pie chart'** from the drop-down box

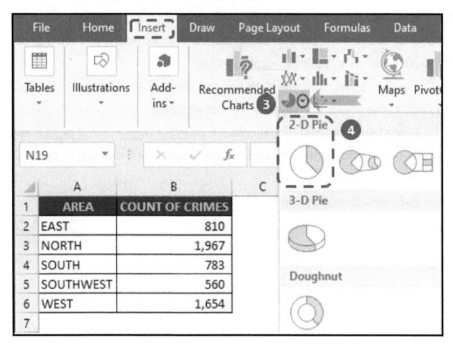

A chart similar to the below should now be displayed:

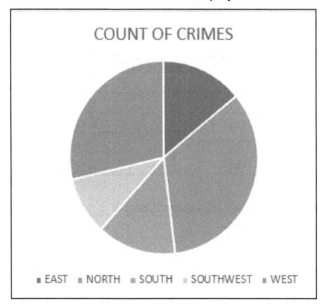

QUICK LAYOUT OPTIONS

5. With the chart selected, from the Ribbon select **Chart Tools : Design**

6. Select the **'Quick Layout'** drop-down arrow

7. Select the <u>first option</u> from the **'Quick Layout'** drop-down list

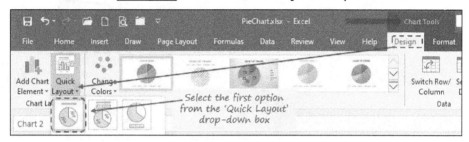

The following Pie Chart should now be displayed:

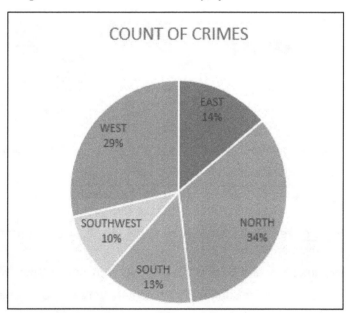

This Pie Chart shows most of the crimes are being committed in the North and West areas of the county.

SPARKLINES

Sparklines are mini *trend charts* contained inside a single cell of a worksheet. Each sparkline represents a single data element and can be displayed in three forms:

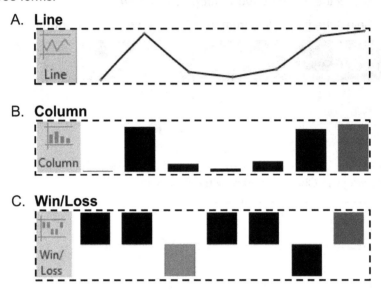

A. **Line**

B. **Column**

C. **Win/Loss**

TIMELINES & SLICERS

Timelines & Slicers are two types of <u>graphical filters</u> and provide an easy and intuitive way for your reporting to be interactive:

- **Timeline:** is a *slider or button filter* allowing for categorization of *individual date values* into months, quarters, or years.

- **Slicers** are *button filters* and allow the user to filter by selecting one or more text values.

These Timelines and Slicers may be used in combination with one another and are ideal for analysts or customers who like to examine data from many different perspectives.

Timeline Example:

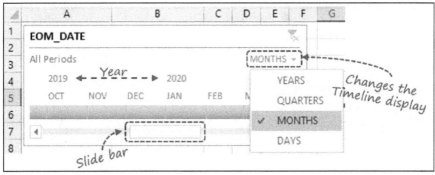

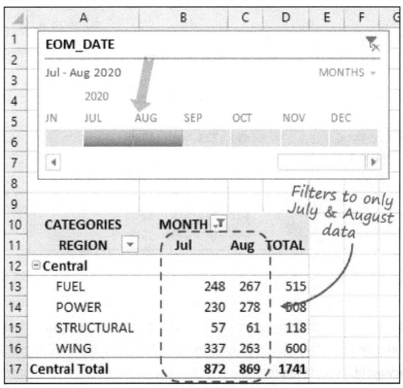

Slicer Example:

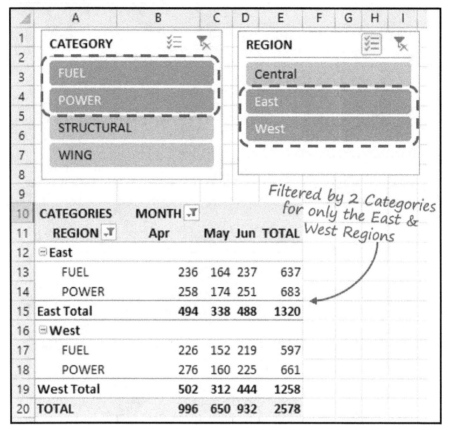

FORMULAS

As the name implies the **'Formula'** tab is all about formulas. Beginning in Chapter 4 we'll go into step-by-step detail on how to use the 25 most commonly used formulas, but for now, the following provides a general overview of the tab features. Some of the most often used commands are:

- Σ AutoSum
- Function Library
- Insert Function
- Formula Auditing

Toolbar is split for easier viewing:

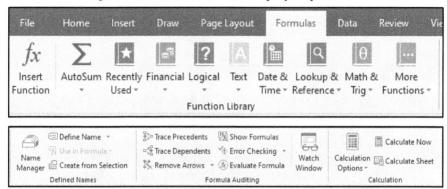

∑ AUTOSUM

While Excel® has hundreds of functions, the challenge is knowing which formula to use when and what the correct syntax is. The **∑ AutoSum** drop-down assists the Excel® beginner by providing the most frequently used functions in a limited list. These are:

1. **Sum** *(adds two or more cells or numbers together)*
2. **Average** *(returns the average number in a range of values)*
3. **Count** *(counts the quantity of numbers in a list of cells)*
4. **Max** *(returns the highest number in a range of values)*
5. **Min** *(returns the lowest number in a range of values)*

You would simply click on the blank cell adjacent to the list of values you want to calculate, click the **∑ AutoSum** drop-down arrow, and select one of the above functions.

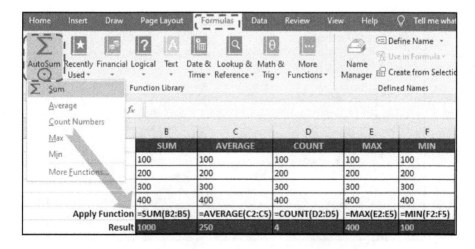

In chapters 4 - 6 we'll go into step-by-step detail on how to use Σ **AutoSum.**

INSERT FUNCTION & FUNCTION LIBRARY

Insert Function & **Function Library** are useful if you already have an understanding of the function you need, but do not know the correct syntax.

For example, let's say you wanted to use the '**VLOOKUP**' formula, but couldn't remember how to enter the precise function arrangement.

A. Place your cursor in the cell you want to apply the formula

B. From the Ribbon select **Formulas : Insert Function**

C. Enter the function name you want find in the box: '**Search for a function:**'

D. Click the '**Go**' button

E. **'Select a function:'**

F. Click the '**OK**' button

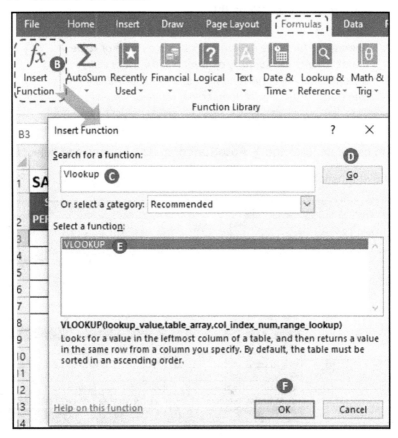

The Function Arguments dialogue box will appear to assist you with

entering the correct syntax:

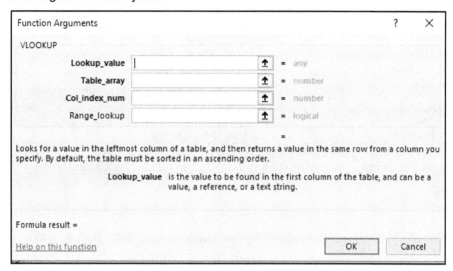

In chapter 11 we review step-by-step on how to use the **VLOOKUP function.**

Similarly, you may use the **Function Library.** For example, if you wanted to

apply an **'IF'** function:

- From the Ribbon select **Formulas : Logical** *(drop-down arrow)*
- From the drop-down list, select the option **'IF'**

The Function Arguments dialogue box will appear to assist you with entering

the correct syntax for the **'IF'** formula:

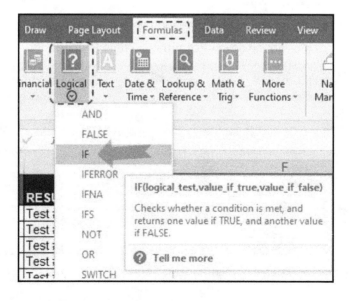

FORMULA AUDITING

The Formula Auditing buttons graphically display, with blue arrows, all the cells a formula *is referencing* or all of the formulas (cells) the selected function *is dependent* on. A very useful feature when you need to troubleshoot or validate a formula is calculating correctly.

FEATURE	DEFINITION
Trace **Precedents**	Traces and displays graphically, with blue arrows, all of the cells a formula *is referencing*
Trace **Dependents**	Displays graphically, with blue arrows, all of the formulas (cells) the selected function is **dependent on**

Examples:

Trace **Precedents**
The formula in cell **'B3'** is *including values* in **cells 'A2', 'A4', & 'A5'**:

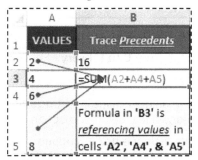

To use this feature:

    A. Select the cell containing the formula you want to audit

    B. From the Ribbon select **Formulas : Trace Precedents**

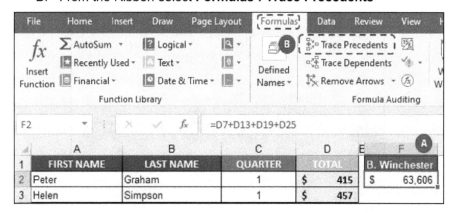

A similar type of graphic should appear:

| F2 | | ⋮ | ✕ | ✓ | ƒx | =D7+D13+D19+D25 ◄ - - - - - - - - - - - |

◢	A	B	C	D	E	F
1	FIRST NAME	LAST NAME	QUARTER	TOTAL		B. Winchester
2	Peter	Graham	1	$ 415	$	63,606
3	Helen	Simpson	1	$ 457		
4	Jack	Smith	1	$ 343		
5	Alex	Steller	1	$ 502		
6	Joe	Tanner	1	$ 377		
7	Billy	Winchester	1	$ 552		
8	Peter	Graham	2	$ 3,125		
9	Helen	Simpson	2	$ 4,062		
10	Jack	Smith	2	$ 1,849		
11	Alex	Steller	2	$ 5,281		
12	Joe	Tanner	2	$ 2,404		
13	Billy	Winchester	2	$ 6,865		
14	Peter	Graham	3	$ 5,969		
15	Helen	Simpson	3	$ 6,785		
16	Jack	Smith	3	$ 2,653		
17	Alex	Steller	3	$ 13,431		
18	Joe	Tanner	3	$ 3,980		
19	Billy	Winchester	3	$ 16,558		
20	Peter	Graham	4	$ 13,199		
21	Helen	Simpson	4	$ 8,954		
22	Jack	Smith	4	$ 5,494		
23	Alex	Steller	4	$ 31,711		
24	Joe	Tanner	4	$ 8,516		
25	Billy	Winchester	4	$ 39,631		

Trace **Dependents**

The formula in cell **'C3'** is _dependent_ on the formula in **'B3'**:

◢	A	B	C
1	VALUES	Trace _Precedents_	Trace _Dependents_
2	2	16	20
3	4	=SUM(A2+A4+A5)	=B3*A3
4	6		
			Formula in 'C3' is
			dependent on the
5	8		formula in 'B3'

To use this feature:

A.   Select the cell containing the formula you want to audit

B.   From the Ribbon select **Formulas : Trace Dependents**

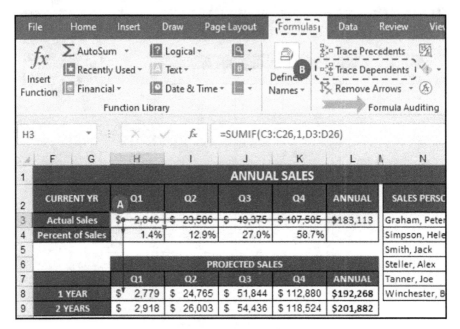

- We can see that cells **'H4', 'H8', & 'L4'** are *dependent* on cell **'H3'**

- Therefore, if you were to remove this formula, it would adversely affect other formulas in this spreadsheet

---

To **remove the arrows**, there are two options:

- From the Ribbon select **Formulas : Remove Arrows** *or*

- **Save** the spreadsheet

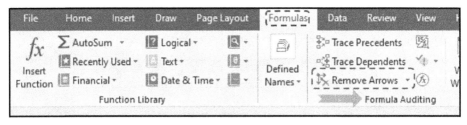

DATA

While Excel's main function is to perform calculations, it's also a very powerful tool for analysis. Within the **'Data'** tab resides the ability to sort, filter, and group information. Forecasting and statistical evaluation may be employed, as well as a variety of sub-totaling options.

As technology has advanced over the years, there's been increased demand to import, transform, and combine data not only from Excel®, but also from external applications. As such, Microsoft® has responded with robust data collection and aggregation capabilities available within the **'Data'** tab.

Indeed, the **'Data'** tab holds some of Excel's most formidable functionality. In this chapter, we'll review just a few of these features:

- Sort
- Filter
- Subtotal

Toolbar is split for easier viewing:

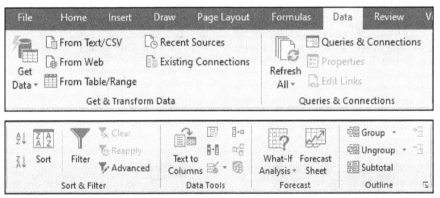

HOW TO SORT AND FILTER RECORDS

We'll begin by learning how to sort records. Sorting allows you to organize your data into a different order by changing the sequence of rows in a spreadsheet to either ***ascending (A – Z alphabetical)*** or ***descending (Z-A reverse alphabetical).*** Thus, making analysis easier by grouping like data.

WEB ADDRESS & FILE NAME FOR EXERCISE:

https://bentonbooks.wixsite.com/bentonbooks/excel-2019
SortingAndFiltering.xlsx

Step-By-Step Examples:

DATA SORTING (STEP-BY-STEP EXAMPLE)

Sample data, due to space limitations **the entire data set is not displayed**.

	A	B	C	D
1	FIRST NAME	LAST NAME	QUARTER	TOTAL
2	Helen	Simpson	1	$ 457
3	Helen	Simpson	2	$ 4,062
4	Helen	Simpson	3	$ 6,785
5	Helen	Simpson	4	$ 8,954
6	Billy	Winchester	1	$ 552
7	Billy	Winchester	2	$ 6,865
8	Billy	Winchester	3	$ 16,558
9	Billy	Winchester	4	$ 39,631
10	Peter	Graham	1	$ 415
11	Peter	Graham	2	$ 3,125
12	Peter	Graham	3	$ 5,969
25	Joe	Tanner	4	$ 8,516

1. Open the spreadsheet SortingAndFiltering.xlsx

2. Select cells **'A1:D25'**

3. From the Ribbon select **Data : Sort**

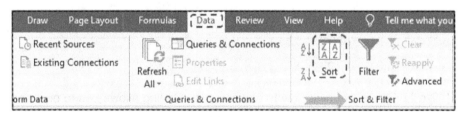

The following dialogue box should appear:

4. In the **'Sort by'** drop-down box:
   - Select **'LAST NAME'** *(this is the underline primary sort)*
   - For the **'Order'** drop-down box select **'A to Z'**

5. Click the **'Add Level'** button
   - A new option called **'Then by'** will appear

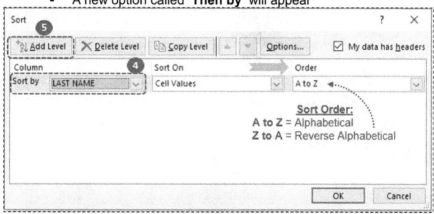

6. In the **'Then by'** drop-down box:
   - Select **'FIRST NAME'** *(this is the secondary sort)*
   - For the **'Order'** drop-down box select **'A to Z'**

7. Click the **'OK'** button

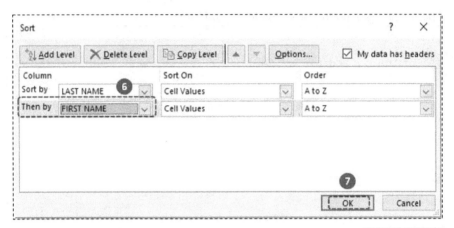

You now have a list in alphabetical order by last name. Due to space limitations **the entire data set is not displayed**.

	A	B	C	D
1	**FIRST NAME**	**LAST NAME**	**QUARTER**	**TOTAL**
2	Peter	Graham	1	$ 415
3	Peter	Graham	2	$ 3,125
4	Peter	Graham	3	$ 5,969
5	Peter	Graham	4	$ 13,199
6	Helen	Simpson	1	$ 457
7	Helen	Simpson	2	$ 4,062
8	Helen	Simpson	3	$ 6,785
9	Helen	Simpson	4	$ 8,954
22	Billy	Winchester	1	$ 552
23	Billy	Winchester	2	$ 6,865
24	Billy	Winchester	3	$ 16,558
25	Billy	Winchester	4	$ 39,631

Additional Information:

NOTE: Excel® allows you to sort any range of cells. If the check box **'My data has headers'** is _unselected,_ the **'Sort by'** drop-down options will appear as:
- ✓ Column A
- ✓ Column B
- ✓ Etc.

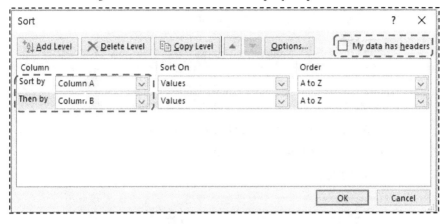

AUTOFILTER (STEP-BY-STEP EXAMPLE)

Next, we'll review how to filter data, as this enables the user to focus on specific areas of interest. In addition to providing easy navigation to specific records in a list. You may also use filtering to display or hide values in a spreadsheet.

The auto **'Filter'** command turns each column heading into a drop-down box in which you can apply *filtering criteria*.

1. Open the spreadsheet SortingAndFiltering.xlsx

2. Select cells **'A1:D1'**

3. From the Ribbon select **Data : Filter**

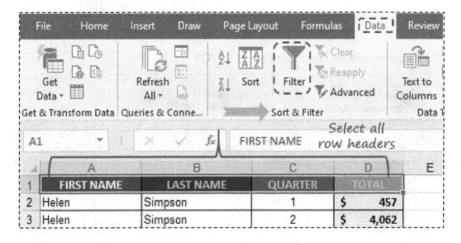

The following drop-down arrows should appear for each column heading:

	A	B	C	D
1	FIRST NAME ▼	LAST NAME ▼	QUARTER ▼	TOTAL ▼
2	Helen	Simpson	1	$ 457
3	Helen	Simpson	2	$ 4,062

4. Click the down-arrow for **column 'C'** (QUARTER)

5. Uncheck the **(Select All)** box and click the box for Q1 **'1'**

6. Click the **'OK'** button

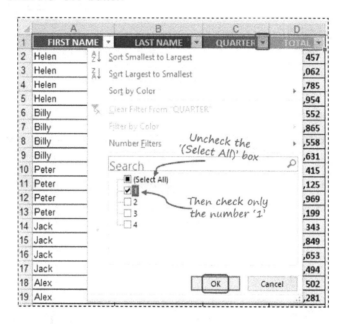

The following will be displayed, sales for **'Q1'**

	A	B	C	D
1	FIRST NAME ▼	LAST NAME ▼	QUARTER ▼	TOTAL ▼
2	Helen	Simpson	1	$ 457
6	Billy	Winchester	1	$ 552
10	Peter	Graham	1	$ 415
14	Jack	Smith	1	$ 343
18	Alex	Steller	1	$ 502
22	Joe	Tanner	1	$ 377

To **remove the filter**

7. Click the down-arrow for **column 'C'** (QUARTER)

8. Select the option **C̲lear Filter From "QUARTER"**

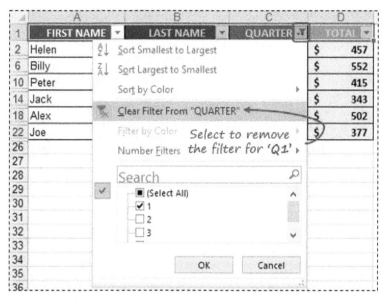

9. Click the down-arrow for **column 'D'** (TOTAL)

10. Click the option **'Number F̲ilters'**

11. From the **'Number F̲ilters'** menu, select the option **'G̲reater Than...'**

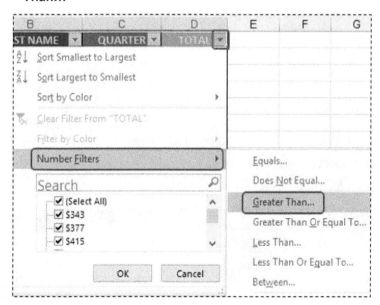

The following prompt will appear,

> 12. Enter **3000** in the box next to *'is greater than'*
>
> 13. Click the **'OK'** button

FIRST NAME ▼	LAST NAME ▼	QUARTER ▼	TOTAL ▼
Helen	Simpson	2	$ 4,062
Helen	Simpson	3	$ 6,785
Helen	Simpson	4	$ 8,954
Billy	Winchester	2	$ 6,865
Billy	Winchester	3	$ 16,558
Billy	Winchester	4	$ 39,631
Peter	Graham *Only sales* 2		$ 3,125
Peter	Graham *>3000 appear* 3		$ 5,969
Peter	Graham	4	$ 13,199
Jack	Smith	4	$ 5,494
Alex	Steller	2	$ 5,281
Alex	Steller	3	$ 13,431
Alex	Steller	4	$ 31,711
Joe	Tanner	3	$ 3,980
Joe	Tanner	4	$ 8,516

SUBTOTAL

In the below illustration, we'll apply a subtotal function to a spreadsheet based on specific criteria. *Your spreadsheet must contain numeric data to use the feature.*

Example:

Using the SortingAndFiltering.xlsx spreadsheet to subtotal by **LAST NAME**.

A. Sort the spreadsheet by Last Name in ascending (A – Z alphabetical) order _and_ Quarter in (Smallest to Largest) order

B. Select all records _(including the header row)_

C. From the Ribbon select **Data : Subtotal**

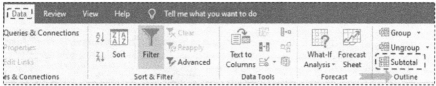

The following dialogue box will appear:

D. Using the following subtotaling criteria:
- At each change in: **'LAST NAME'**
- Use function: **'Sum'**
- Add subtotal to: **'Total'**

E. Click the '**OK**' button

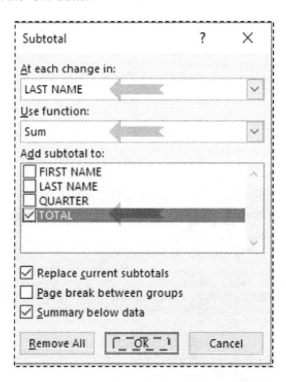

The following subtotal rows have been added to the spreadsheet **_Note:_** *the grouping buttons in the left margin:*

1 2 3		A	B	C	D
	1	**FIRST NAME**	**LAST NAME**	**QUARTER**	**TOTAL**
	2	Peter	Graham	1	$ 415
	3	Peter	Graham	2	$ 3,125
	4	Peter	Graham	3	$ 5,969
	5	Peter	Graham	4	$ 13,199
	6		**Graham Total**		$ 22,708
	7	Helen	Simpson	1	$ 457
	8	Helen	Simpson	2	$ 4,062
	9	Helen	Simpson	3	$ 6,785
	10	Helen	Simpson	4	$ 8,954
	11		**Simpson Total**		$ 20,258

Example of **'LAST NAME'** subtotaled and grouped **(level 2)**:

1 2 3		A	B	C	D
	1	**FIRST NAME**	**LAST NAME**	**QUARTER**	**TOTAL**
+	6		**Graham Total**		$ 22,708
+	11		**Simpson Total**		$ 20,258
+	16		**Smith Total**		$ 10,339
+	21		**Steller Total**		$ 50,925
+	26		**Tanner Total**		$ 15,276
+	31		**Winchester Total**		$ 63,606
	32				
	33		**Grand Total**		$ 183,113

To ungroup click the **level 3** button

REVIEW

The **'REVIEW'** tab is primarily used for editing and preventing the deliberate or inadvertent changing of the spreadsheet contents. Commands include:

- Spellcheck & Thesaurus
- Protecting worksheets & workbooks

Toolbar is split for easier viewing:

SPELLCHECK & THESAURUS

To access the **Thesaurus**:
> Click the '**Thesaurus**' button _or_
> From your keyboard press shortcut keys (**Shift+F7**)

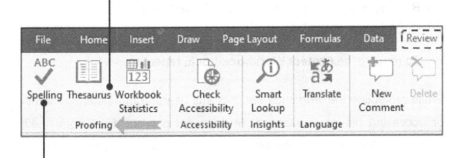

To check the **spelling of text** in your worksheet:
> Click the '**Spelling**' button _or_
> From your keyboard press shortcut key **F7**

PROTECTING WORKSHEETS & WORKBOOKS

To avoid someone or yourself from accidentally deleting or changing content (including formulas), you can protect the worksheet(s) within a workbook or the workbook file itself.

A. From the Ribbon select **Review : Protect Workbook**

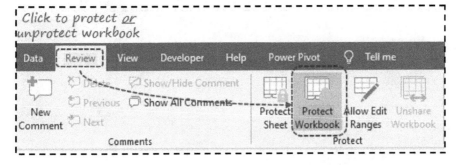

The following dialogue box will appear:

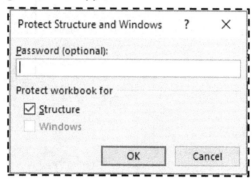

    B. Optionally, enter a **Password** or leave blank

    C. Click the **'OK'** button

- To remove the **Protect Workbook Lock**, repeat step #A

While protecting the *workbook file* prevents users from deleting, renaming, or accessing hidden worksheets, it does not prevent them from making changes to the content of the worksheets themselves. Therefore, we must complete additional steps:

    A. Select the worksheet

    B. From the Ribbon select **Review : Protect Sheet**

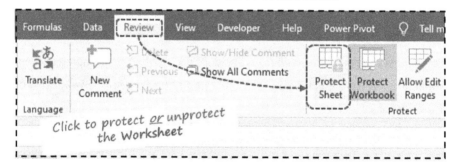

The following dialogue box will appear:

C. You may enter a password or leave blank

D. A good best practice is to leave the first two check boxes selected:
   - Select locked cells
   - Select unlocked cells

These will allow users to click on cells and scroll, but not change any content

E. Click the **'OK'** button

If a user tries to modify the sheet, they will receive the following message:

- To **unprotect** the sheet from the Ribbon select **Review : Unprotect Sheet**

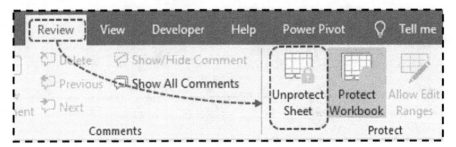

VIEW

The **'VIEW'** tab commands are useful when you need to have different display options or need to quickly hide confidential spreadsheets, such as those related to Human Resources or Medical files.

Toolbar is split for easier viewing:

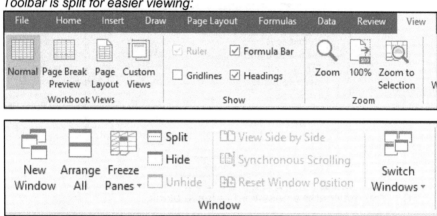

SPLIT (SCREEN)

Often, when working with large amounts data, you may want to analyze two records that are not close in order, this is where the **'Split'** command is helpful.

Example:

If I want to <u>compare</u> *row 205* to *row 1,036*.
- Select the first row below row 205, in this case row 206
- From the Ribbon select **View : Split**

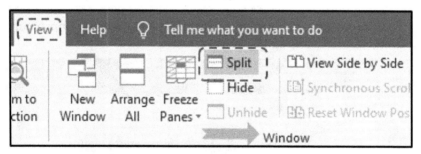

I can now compare two records that are not close in order:

205	Record 314	204	204.25	204.5	204.75	205	205.25	205.5	205.75
206	Record 315	205	205.25	205.5	205.75	206	206.25	206.5	206.75
1035	Record 1144	1034	1034.25	1034.5	1034.75	1035	1035.25	1035.5	1035.75
1036	Record 1145	1035	1035.25	1035.5	1035.75	1036	1036.25	1036.5	1036.75

FREEZE PANES

'Freeze Panes' keeps the column and rows you specify locked when scrolling. This is especially helpful, when working with spreadsheets with a lot of rows and columns.

Example:

To always see the column headings *(row 1)* and REGION *(column 'A')*:

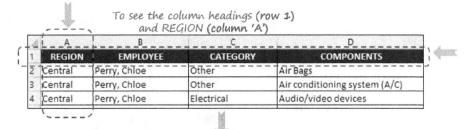

after scrolling to see more data

Missing the column headings **(row 1)** and REGION (column 'A')

	C	D	E	F	G
10	Other	Console	31 January 2019	$ 13	$ 12
11	Structural	Doors	31 January 2019	$ 13	$ 11
12	Electrical	Electrical supply system	31 January 2019	$ 13	$ 11
13	Electrical	Electrical switches	31 January 2019	$ 13	$ 11

Applying the **'Freeze Panes'** command to cell **'B2'**:

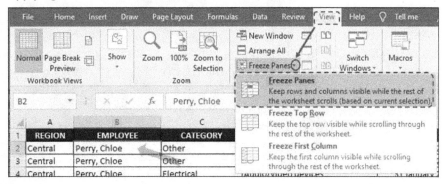

I can now see the column headings and the record number for this row when scrolling down and to the left:

A REGION	D COMPONENTS	E EOM_DATE	F PLAN	G SALES
2858 West	Console	30 June 2019	$ 13	$ 13
2859 West	Doors	30 June 2019	$ 13	$ 12
2860 West	Electrical supply system	30 June 2019	$ 13	$ 14

HELP & TELL ME WHAT YOU WANT TO DO

If you have a question about how to perform an action in Excel®, the two easiest ways to get more information is from the **'Help'** tab or the '**Tell me what you want to do'** search feature.

Help tab

A. From the Ribbon select **Help : Help** (question mark (?) circle button)
B. Enter your question in the search box, i.e. *"how to insert a formula"*
C. Click the magnifying glass
D. Results are returned

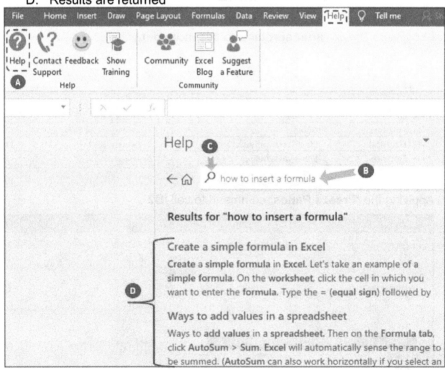

Tell me what you want to do search feature

A. From the Ribbon select **Tell me what you want to do** (light bulb)

B. Enter your question in the search box, i.e. *"how to insert a formula"*
C. Click the question mark (?) circle

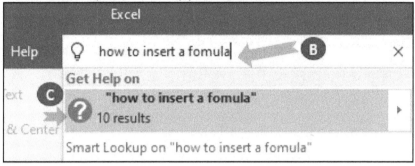

D. Results are returned

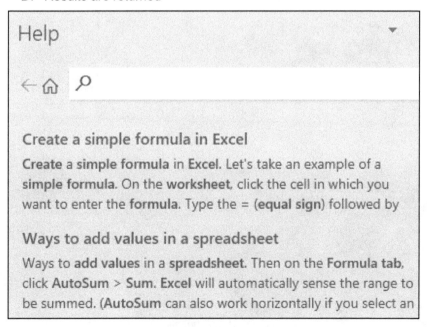

Help

Create a simple formula in Excel

Create a simple formula in Excel. Let's take an example of a simple formula. On the worksheet, click the cell in which you want to enter the formula. Type the = (equal sign) followed by

Ways to add values in a spreadsheet

Ways to add values in a spreadsheet. Then on the Formula tab, click AutoSum > Sum. Excel will automatically sense the range to be summed. (AutoSum can also work horizontally if you select an

SECTION ~ THREE

25 EXCEL STEP-BY-STEP FORMULA EXAMPLES

CHAPTER 4

BASIC FORMULAS

Excel's primary purpose is to perform calculations. From simple arithmetic to multifaceted expressions, these computations are inserted into a cell in the form of a **formula** or **function** and require the appropriate **syntax**.

IS THERE A DIFFERENCE BETWEEN A *FORMULA* AND A *FUNCTION*?

In Excel®, the terms *'formula'* and *'function'* are used interchangeably. Most users do not differentiate between the two. Even Microsoft® labels the tab **'Formulas'** when really it is more representative of functions.

The subtle difference is a *'function'* is entered with a *name*, such as *'SUM'*, *'AVERAGE'*, or *'VLOOKUP'* and typically involves the evaluation of other cells. A *'formula'* may be entered with an operator like (+, -, * or /) and does not require the inclusion of cells. Below is an example:

```
Formula:  =2+2         result is 4
Function: =SUM(B2:B3)  result is 4
```

	A	B
1	Formula	Function
2	2	2
3	2	2
4	=2+2	=SUM(B2:B3)

From a communication standpoint, it is much easier to say 'formula', since this is what most people are familiar with. **Therefore, in this book, the term 'formula' is used more often.**

FUNCTION

> A **function** in Excel® is a predefined formula. An example of a function name is 'SUM'.

FORMULA

> A **formula** calculates numbers or evaluates the contents of one or more cells.

> **Syntax** in Excel® refers to the arrangement or order of a formula or function. All formulas & functions begin with the equal sign (=) followed by numbers or the function's name.

Below are the fundamental formulas most people learn first.

ARITHMETIC APPLICATION	OPERATOR	DEFINITION
Sum (Addition)	**+**	Adds two or more cells or numbers together
Subtraction	**-**	Subtracts two or more cells or numbers
Multiplication	*	Multiplies two or more cells or numbers
Division	/	Divides two or more cells or numbers

Step-By-Step Examples:

SUM (ADDITION)

1. Begin by creating a new blank Excel® spreadsheet:
   - From your keyboard press shortcut keys **(CTRL+N)** *or*
   - Click the **'New Document'** icon from the **'Quick Access'** toolbar:

2. Enter the following numbers into **column 'A'**
   - Cell **'A1'** enter the number **2**
   - Cell **'A2'** enter the number **3**
   - Cell **'A3'** enter the number **1**
   - Cell **'A4'** enter the number **2**

The spreadsheet should look similar to the following:

	A
1	2
2	3
3	1
4	2
5	

3. Click cell **'A5'**

4. From the Ribbon select the tab '**Formulas**'

5. Click the ∑ **AutoSum** drop-down arrow

6. Select ∑ **Sum**

7. Press the '**Enter**' button on your keyboard

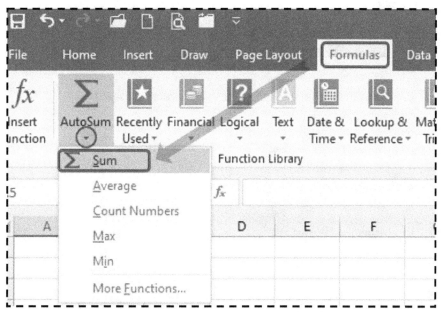

The result should be **8**:

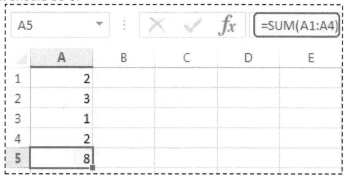

Alternatively, you may also **type the following into cell 'A5'**:

1. Enter the **equal =** symbol from your keyboard

2. Type **sum(**

3. Select (highlight) rows **'A1:A4'**

4. Press the **'Enter'** [Enter ↵] button on your keyboard

SUBTRACTION

Using the same the sample data as the 'Sum' section:

1. Select cell **'B3'**

2. Enter the **equal =** [= +] symbol from your keyboard

3. Click cell 'A2'

4. Enter the **minus -** [- -] symbol from your keyboard

5. Click cell **'A3'**

6. Press the **'Enter'** [Enter ↵] button on your keyboard

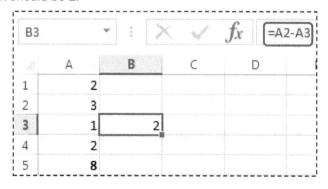

The result should be **2**:

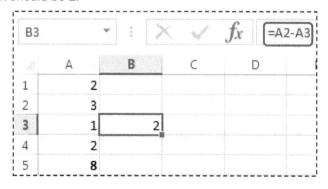

MULTIPLICATION

Using the same the sample data as the 'Sum' section:

1. Select cell **'B4'**

2. Enter the **equal =** symbol from your keyboard

3. Click cell '**A4'**

4. Enter the **asterisk *** symbol from your keyboard (shift key + 8 key)

5. Click cell '**A1'**

6. Press the **'Enter'** button on your keyboard

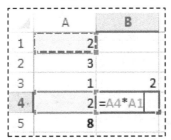

The result should be **4**:

DIVISION

Using the same the sample data as the 'Sum' section:

1. Select cell **'C4'**

2. Enter the **equal =** symbol from your keyboard

3. Click cell '**B4**'

4. Enter the **forward slash /** ![?/] symbol from your keyboard

5. Click cell '**B3**'

6. Press the '**Enter**' ![Enter] button on your keyboard

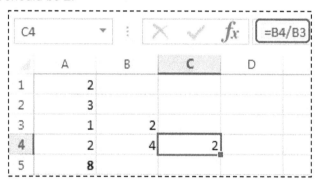

The result should be **2**:

ADDITIONAL EXAMPLES:

	A	B	C	D	E
1	ARITHMETIC APPLICATION	EXAMPLE DATA	EXAMPLE DATA	FORMULA	RESULT
2	Sum	2	3	=SUM(B2:C2)	5
3	Sum	-	-	=SUM(2+3)	5
4	Sum	-	-	=2+3	5
6	Subtraction	3	1	=B6-C6	2
7	Subtraction	-	-	=3-1	2
9	Multiplication	7	9	=B9*C9	63
10	Multiplication	-	-	=7*9	63
12	Division	4	2	=B12/C12	2
13	Division	-	-	=4/2	2

	A	B	C	D
1	ADDING NUMBERS TOGETHER	SUM & MULTIPLICATION	SUM & DIVISION	
2	2	2	2	
3	3	3	3	
4	7	7	7	
5	4	4	4	
6	=A2+A3+A4+A5	=SUM(B2:B5)*2	=SUM(C2:C5)/2	FORMULA
7	16	32	8	RESULT

CHAPTER 5

CALCULATING AVERAGES

FUNCTION	DEFINITION
Average	Returns the average number in a range of values, does not include text in the evaluation

Quick Example:

```
Syntax:
AVERAGE(number1, [number2], ...)

Number1 is required, subsequent numbers are optional
```

A4	▼	:	✕	✓	*fx*	=AVERAGE(A2:A3)

	A	B	C	D	E
1	**SALES**				
2	$100				
3	$200				
4	$150				

Step-By-Step Example:

AVERAGE FUNCTION

1. Begin by creating a new blank Excel® spreadsheet:
   - From your keyboard press shortcut keys **(CTRL+N)** <u>or</u>
   - Click the **'New Document'** icon from the **'Quick Access'** toolbar:

2. Enter the following numbers into **column 'A'**
   - Cell **'A1'** enter the label **'SALES'**
   - Cell **'A2'** enter the number **100**
   - Cell **'A3'** enter the number **200**
   - Cell **'A4'** enter the number **300**
   - Cell **'A5'** enter the number **400**

The spreadsheet should look similar to the following:

	A
1	**SALES**
2	100
3	200
4	300
5	400

3. Select cell **'A6'**

4. From the Ribbon select the '**Formulas**' tab

5. Click the Σ **AutoSum** drop-down arrow

6. Select **'Average'**

7. Press the **'Enter'** button on your keyboard

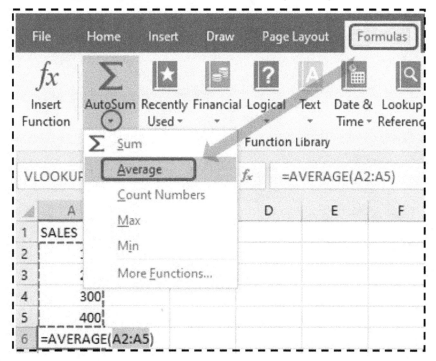

The result should be an average of **250**:

A6			×	✓	f_x	=AVERAGE(A2:A5)

	A	B	C	D	E
1	**SALES**				
2	100				
3	200				
4	300				
5	400				
6	250				

Alternatively, you may also enter the following into cell **'A6'**:

1. Enter the **equal =** ⎡ + ⎤ ⎣ = ⎦ symbol from your keyboard

2. Type **average(**

3. Select (highlight) rows **'A2:A5'**

4. Press the **'Enter'** ⎡ Enter ⎤ ⎣ ← ⎦ button on your keyboard

CHAPTER 6

DETERMINING THE MINIMUM & MAXIMUM NUMBER IN A LIST

FUNCTION	DEFINITION
MIN	Returns the lowest number in a range of values, does not include text in the evaluation
MAX	Returns the largest number in a range of values, does not include text in the evaluation

Quick Examples: MIN & MAX

```
Syntax:
MIN(number1, [number2], ...)
Number1 is required, subsequent numbers are optional
```

B2	▼	:	✕	✓	*fx*	=MIN(A2:A4)

◢	A	B	C	D	E
1	LIST	MIN	MAX		
2	1	1			
3	2				
4	3				

```
MAX(number1, [number2], ...)
Number1 is required, subsequent numbers are optional
```

C2	▼	:	✕	✓	*fx*	=MAX(A2:A4)

◢	A	B	C	D	E
1	LIST	MIN	MAX		
2	1	1	3		
3	2				
4	3				

WEB ADDRESS & FILE NAME FOR EXERCISE:
https://bentonbooks.wixsite.com/bentonbooks/excel-2019
MinAndMaxFormulas.xlsx

Step-By-Step Example:
Sample data, due to space limitations **the entire data set is not displayed**.

	A	B	C	D	E	F	G
1	SALES PERSON FIRST NAME	SALES PERSON LAST NAME	QUARTER	TOTAL		BEST SALES	WORST SALES
2	Jack	Smith	1	$ 343			
3	Jack	Smith	2	$ 1,849			
4	Jack	Smith	3	$ 2,653			
5	Jack	Smith	4	$ 5,494			
6	Joe	Tanner	1	$ 377			
7	Joe	Tanner	2	$ 2,404			
8	Joe	Tanner	3	$ 3,980			
9	Joe	Tanner	4	$ 39,631			
25	Billy	Winchester	4	$ 8,516			

MAX

1. Open the spreadsheet MinAndMaxFormulas.xlsx

2. Place your cursor in cell **'F2'**

3. From the Ribbon select the **'Formulas'** tab

4. Click the Σ **AutoSum** drop-down arrow

5. Select **'Max'**

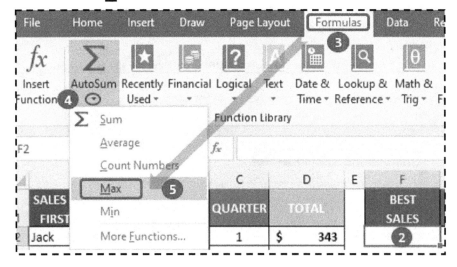

6. Select **column 'D'**

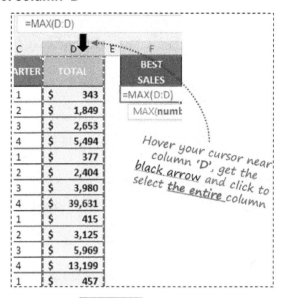

7. Press the **'Enter'** button on your keyboard

MIN

8. Place your cursor in cell **'G2'**

9. From the Ribbon select the **'Formulas'** tab

10. Click the **Σ AutoSum** drop-down arrow

11. Select **'Min'**

12. Select **column 'D'**

13. Press the **'Enter'** button on your keyboard

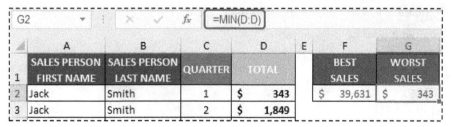

The results should be:

39,631 Best Sales Results
  343 Worst Sales Results

Alternatively, you may also enter the following into cell **'F2'**:

1. Enter the **equal =** symbol from your keyboard

2. Type **max(**

3. Select column **'D'**

4. Press the **'Enter'** button on your keyboard

or for **MIN**:

You may enter the following into cell **'G2'**:

1. Enter the **equal =** symbol from your keyboard

2. Type **min(**

3. Select column **'D'**

4. Press the **'Enter'** key on your keyboard

☑ Additional Information:

All the functions reviewed in chapters 4 – 6 may also be accomplished using PivotTables. However, sometimes it is faster to use one of the above formulas when your sample size is small or you're simply providing these results in an email, IM (instant message), or text.

Similarly, these are very useful functions when you want to **double check your results**. It's always worthwhile to validate your numbers to ensure you're not missing any values. By taking just a few extra minutes to verify your calculations, you'll likely catch any mistakes, improve your creditability with customers, and have the confidence to defend your work should it ever be questioned.

CHAPTER 7

BASIC DATE & TIME FUNCTIONS

FUNCTION	DEFINITION
TODAY	Provides **today's date**. *NOTE: this formula will update each day, it is always the current date*
NOW	Provides **today's date** *and* **time**. *NOTE: this formula will update each day, it is always the current date and time*
NETWORKDAYS	Calculates the number of **workdays (Monday – Friday)** between two dates

Quick Examples:

TODAY & NOW (FUNCTIONS)

There are no parameters for the **'Today()'** or **'Now()'** functions.

	A	B
1	FUNCTION	RESULT
2	=TODAY()	11/25/2019
3	=NOW()	11/25/19 1:19 PM

```
Function: =TODAY() result is 11/25/2019
Function:   =NOW() result is 11/25/2019 1:19 PM
```

NETWORKDAYS

> **Syntax:**
>
> NETWORKDAYS(start_date, end_date, [holidays])
>
> **start_date** and **end_date** are required, **holidays** is optional

C2			$\times$	$\checkmark$	f_x	=NETWORKDAYS(A2,B2)

◢	A	B	C	D
1	START DATE	COMPLETION DATE	HOW MANY WORKDAYS?	
2	8/1/2020	10/31/2020	65	

WEB ADDRESS & FILE NAME FOR EXERCISE:
https://bentonbooks.wixsite.com/bentonbooks/excel-2019
NetWorkDays.xlsx

Scenario:

You've been asked to determine how many resources are needed to complete a project by specific date.

- The start of the project is **08/01/2020** and needs to be completed by **10/31/2020**
- The project is estimated to take **1,040 hours**
- Assume each resource would work one **8 hour shift** per day, Monday – Friday

It would take 1 resource 130 days to complete the project including weekends:

$$(1040 \text{ hours } / 8 \text{ hour shift} = 130 \text{ days})$$

Therefore, we know we need more resources, but how many?

Step-By-Step Example:

First, we need to determine how many *workdays* there are between 08/01/2020 and 10/31/2020. Once we know this amount, we can then multiply this value with the number of hours per shift to determine the appropriate total of resources needed to complete the project by 10/31/2020.

1. Open the spreadsheet NetWorkDays.xlsx
2. Place your cursor in cell **'C2'**
3. From the Ribbon select **Formulas : Date & Time** (*drop-down arrow*)

4. From the drop-down list, select the option **'NETWORKDAYS'**

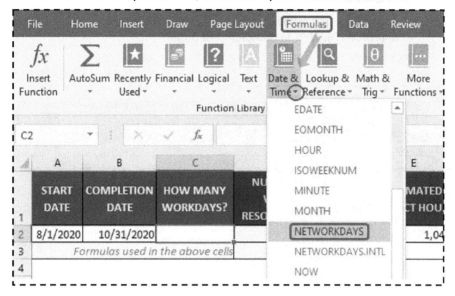

The Function Arguments dialogue box will appear:
- For the **Start_date** click cell 'A2' or enter **A2**
- For the **End_date** click cell 'B2' or enter **B2**
- Click the '**OK**' button

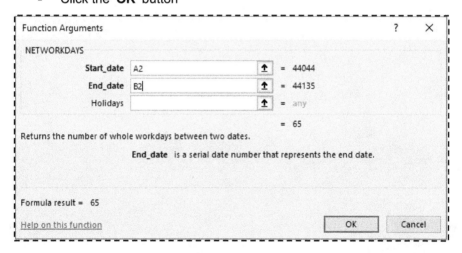

The result is **65 days:**

5. Apply the basic calculations to determine the appropriate amount of resources needed to complete the project

```
(65 Days x 8 hours = 520 hours for 1 Resource)
(1040 hours/520 hours for 1 Resource = 2 Resources Needed)
```

	A	B	C	D	E	F
1	START DATE	COMPLETION DATE	HOW MANY WORKDAYS?	NUMBER OF HOURS WORKED FOR 1 RESOURCE FOR 65 DAYS	ESTIMATED PROJECT HOURS	RESOURCES NEEDED TO COMPLETE BY 10/31/2020
2	8/1/2020	10/31/2020	65	520	1,040	2
3		Formulas used in the above cells		C2*8 = 520		E2/D2 = 2

The result is **2 resources** are needed to complete the project by **10/31/2020.**

CHAPTER 8

FUNCTION	DEFINITION
TEXT	TEXT changes the **appearance** of a number or date to the format you specify using format codes
PROPER	Converts the text of a cell to proper (normal case). Meaning, the first letter of each word is uppercase (capitalized) and the following letters of the same word are lowercase
UPPER	Converts all text characters of a cell to **UPPERCASE** (capitalized)
LOWER	Converts all text characters of a cell to **lowercase**

Quick Examples:

```
TEXT - Syntax:
TEXT(value, format_text)
value required, format_text required
```

⊿	A	B	C
1	DATE	FORMULA	RESULT
2	11/18/2020	=TEXT(B2,"dddd")	Wednesday

```
Syntax:              Syntax:              Syntax:
PROPER(text)         UPPER(text)          LOWER(text)
text is required     text is required     text is required
```

⊿	A	B	C
1	FROM--->	FORMULA	TO
2	apples	=PROPER(A2)	Apples
3	Apples	=UPPER(A3)	APPLES
4	APPLES	=LOWER(A4)	apples

WEB ADDRESS & FILE NAME FOR EXERCISE:
https://bentonbooks.wixsite.com/bentonbooks/excel-2019
TextFunctions.xlsx

Step-By-Step Examples:

TEXT

In our first example, we'll apply the **TEXT** function to format a date value (i.e. 11/1/2020) to the **day of the week** (i.e. Wednesday).

Sample data:

	A	B	C	D
1	DATE	DAY OF WEEK *(long form)*	DATE	DAY OF WEEK *(short form)*
2	11/1/2020		11/1/2020	Sun
3	11/2/2020		11/2/2020	Mon
4	11/3/2020		11/3/2020	Tue
5	11/4/2020		11/4/2020	Wed
6	11/5/2020		11/5/2020	Thu
7	11/6/2020		11/6/2020	Fri
8	11/7/2020		11/7/2020	Sat

1. Open the TextFunctions.xlsx spreadsheet
2. Select the tab named **'TEXT'**

3. Place your cursor in cell **'B2'**
4. From the Ribbon select **Formulas : TEXT** *(drop-down arrow)*
5. From the drop-down list, select the option **'TEXT'**

The Function Arguments dialogue box will appear:
- For the **Value** click cell '**A2**' or enter **A2**
- For the **Format_text** enter **dddd** (*this is the* <u>*format code*</u> *for the day of the week, see page for next page for more codes*)
- Click the '**OK**' button

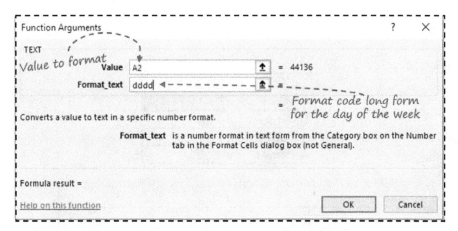

6. Select cell '**B2**' right-click and select '**Copy**' or press **Ctrl+C** on your keyboard

7. Select cells **'B3:B8'** and from your keyboard press shortcut keys (**CTRL+V**)

The result should be as follows:

	A	B	C	D
1	**DATE**	**DAY OF WEEK** *(long form)*	**DATE**	**DAY OF WEEK** *(short form)*
2	11/1/2020	Sunday	11/1/2020	Sun
3	11/2/2020	Monday	11/2/2020	Mon
4	11/3/2020	Tuesday	11/3/2020	Tue
5	11/4/2020	Wednesday	11/4/2020	Wed
6	11/5/2020	Thursday	11/5/2020	Thu
7	11/6/2020	Friday	11/6/2020	Fri
8	11/7/2020	Saturday	11/7/2020	Sat

TEXT FORMAT CODES

More examples of **TEXT** function format codes:

	A	B	C	D	E	F
1	TO DISPLAY	AS	FORMAT CODE	EXAMPLE	FORMULA	RESULT
2	Date	22-07-2020	"dd-mm-yyyy"	11/18/2020	=TEXT(D2,"dd-mm-yyyy")	18-11-2020
3	Date	22 July 2020	"dd mmmm yyyy"	11/18/2020	=TEXT(D3,"dd mmmm yyyy")	18 November 2020
4	Days	Sun–Sat	"ddd"	11/18/2020	=TEXT(D4,"ddd")	Wed
5	Days	Sunday–Saturday	"dddd"	11/18/2020	=TEXT(D5,"dddd")	Wednesday
6	Months	1–12	"m"	11/18/2020	=TEXT(D6,"m")	11
7	Months	Jan–Dec	"mmm"	11/18/2020	=TEXT(D7,"mmm")	Nov
8	Months	January–December	"mmmm"	11/18/2020	=TEXT(D8,"mmmm")	November
9	Years	00–99	"yy"	11/18/2020	=TEXT(D9,"yy")	20
10	Years	1900–9999	"yyyy"	11/18/2020	=TEXT(D10,"yyyy")	2020

For even more format codes please visit Microsoft's website:
https://support.office.com/en-us/article/text-function-20d5ac4d-7b94-49fd-bb38-93d29371225c

PROPER

Sample data:

	A	B	C
1	**CASE**	**FROM**	**TO**
2	**Proper**	aPPLe	
3	**UPPER**	apple	
4	**lower**	APPLE	

1. Select the tab named **'CASE'**

2. Place your cursor in cell **'C2'**

3. From the Ribbon select **Formulas : Text** *(drop-down arrow)*

4. From the drop-down list, select the option **'PROPER'**

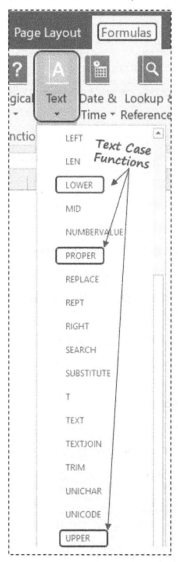

5. In the Function Arguments dialogue box, click cell **'B2'** or enter **B2** in the **'Text'** field

6. Click the **'OK'** button

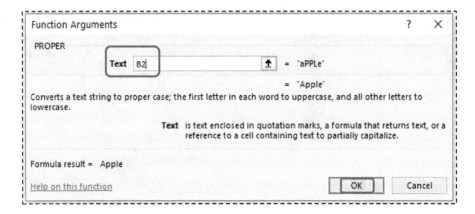

UPPER

1. Place your cursor in cell **'C3'**

2. From the Ribbon select **Formulas : Text** *(drop-down arrow)*

3. From the drop-down list, select the option **'UPPER'**

4. In the Function Arguments dialogue box, click cell **'B3'** or enter **B3** in the **'Text'** field

5. Click the **'OK'** button

LOWER

1. Place your cursor in cell **'C4'**

2. From the Ribbon select **Formulas : Text** *(drop-down arrow)*

3. From the drop-down list, select the option **'LOWER'**

4. In the Function Arguments dialogue box, click cell **'B4'** or enter **B4** in the **'Text'** field

5. Click the **'OK'** button

The result should be as follows:

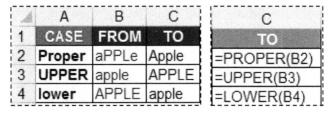

CHAPTER 9

TEXT FUNCTIONS PART 2 – LEN, TRIM, CONCAT, & MID

FUNCTION	DEFINITION
LEN	The LEN function counts the number characters in a cell
TRIM	The TRIM function removes all extraneous spaces from a cell, *except for* single spaces between words
CONCAT / CONCATENATE	CONCAT joins two or more cells together and allows the option to insert additional text into the merged cell
MID	MID Returns a specific number of characters from a text string, starting at a position you specify, based on the number of characters you stipulate

Quick Examples:

Syntax:
LEN(text)
text is required

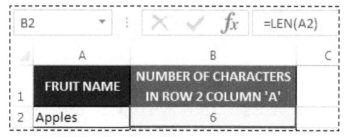

Syntax:
TRIM(text)
text is required

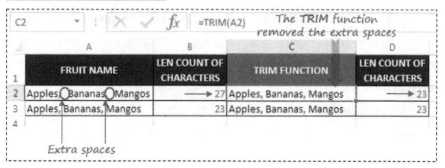

Function Syntax:	Function Syntax:	
CONCAT(text)	CONCATENATE(text)	*Excel version*
text is required	**text is required**	*2013 & earlier*

	A	B	C	D
1	SALES PERSON FIRST NAME	SALES PERSON LAST NAME	FORMULA	CONCAT merged cells 'B2 and 'A2'. Last Name, followed by a comma and space, then First Name
2	Jack	Smith	=CONCAT(B2,", ",A2)	Smith, Jack

Syntax:
MID(text, start_num, num_chars)
All arguments are required

	A	B	C	D
1	SALES PERSON FIRST NAME	SALES PERSON LAST NAME	FORMULA	Started in positon 1 of cell 'A2' and returned the 1st character
2	Jack	Smith	=MID(A2,1,1)	J

WEB ADDRESS & FILE NAME FOR EXERCISE:
https://bentonbooks.wixsite.com/bentonbooks/excel-2019
TextFunctions.xlsx

Scenario:

You've been given a report that was created by a Database Administrator (DBA). The DBA created the file by running a query in a database, exporting the results into a .CSV file, and then opened and re-saved the report as an Excel® file.

As the Business Analyst, you're attempting to reconcile the data using a PivotTable. In your analysis, you've discovered *some* cell values *"appear"* to be the same, but are being returned as two separate records in your results.

You use the **LEN function** to troubleshoot why you're getting two separate records in your results for what appear to be the same value.

Appear the same, but are reporting as separate values

Row Labels ▾	Sum of FRUIT SALES
Apples	100
Apples	500
Kiwi	600
Oranges	600
Grand Total	1800

Step-By-Step Examples:

LEN

Sample data:

	A	B
1	FRUIT NAME	FRUIT SALES
2	Apples	100
3	Kiwi	100
4	Oranges	100
5	Apples	200
6	Kiwi	200
7	Oranges	200
8	Apples	300
9	Kiwi	300
10	Oranges	300

1. Open the TextFunctions.xlsx spreadsheet

2. Select the tab named **'LEN'**

| TEXT | CASE | **LEN** | TRIM | CONCAT | MID |

3. Sort the results by **'Fruit Name'** in **Ascending order** *(please see chapter 3 page 50 for instructions on Data Sorting)*

Sort Column 'A' in
Ascending order

	A	B
1	**FRUIT NAME**	**FRUIT SALES**
2	Apples	100
3	Kiwi	100
4	Oranges	100
5	Apples	200
6	Kiwi	200
7	Oranges	200
8	Apples	300
9	Kiwi	300
10	Oranges	300
11		

4. Click cell '**C2**'

	A	B	C	
1	**FRUIT NAME**	**FRUIT SALES**	**LEN FUNCTION**	
2	Apples	100		
3	Apples	200		
4	Apples	300		
5	Kiwi	100		
6	Kiwi	200		
7	Kiwi	300		
8	Oranges	100		
9	Oranges	200		
10	Oranges	300		
11				

5. From the Ribbon select **Formulas : Text : LEN**

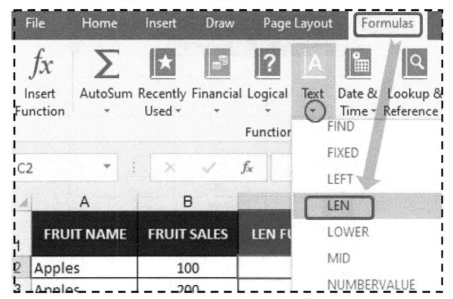

The Function Arguments dialogue box will appear:

6. Click on cell '**A2**' or enter '**A2**' in the **Text** field

7. Click the '**OK**' button

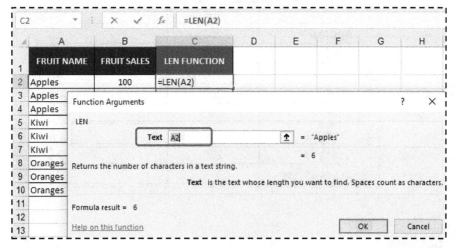

8. Select cell '**C2**' right-click and select '**Copy**' or press **Ctrl+C** on your keyboard

9. Select cells '**C3:C10**' and from your keyboard press shortcut keys (**CTRL+V**)

There appears to be an extra space in cells '**A3**' & '**A4**' *after the fruit name* '*Apple*'

⬚	A	B	C
1	**FRUIT NAME**	**FRUIT SALES**	**LEN FUNCTION**
2	Apples	100	6
3	Apples	200	7
4	Apples	300	7
5	Kiwi	100	4
6	Kiwi	200	4
7	Kiwi	300	4
8	Oranges	100	7
9	Oranges	200	7
10	Oranges	300	7

10. In cells **'A3 & A4'** at the end of the fruit name **'Apple',** remove the extra space

This will resolve the error:

⬚	A	B	C
1	**FRUIT NAME**	**FRUIT SALES**	**LEN FUNCTION**
2	**Apples**	**100**	6
3	**Apples**	**200**	6
4	**Apples**	**300**	6
5	Kiwi	100	4
6	Kiwi	200	4
7	Kiwi	300	4
8	Oranges	100	7
9	Oranges	200	7
10	Oranges	300	7

TRIM

Scenario:

You've been given an Excel® report generated by another application. Upon review, you see the content in the cells contains extra spaces between and after the words. To make the report usable for analysis and presentation you need to remove the extraneous spaces. You decide to use the **TRIM function** to remove the spaces.

Below is an example of the report showing what must be corrected in order to create a Pivot Table report.

Sample data:

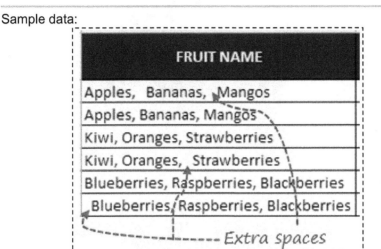

1. Select the tab named **'TRIM'**

2. Click cell '**C2**'

	A	B	C
1	FRUIT NAME	LEN COUNT OF CHARACTERS	TRIM FUNCTION
2	Apples, Bananas, Mangos	27	
3	Apples, Bananas, Mangos	23	
4	Kiwi, Oranges, Strawberries	27	
5	Kiwi, Oranges, Strawberries	29	
6	Blueberries, Raspberries, Blackberries	38	
7	Blueberries, Raspberries, Blackberries	40	

3. From the Ribbon select **Formulas : Text : TRIM**

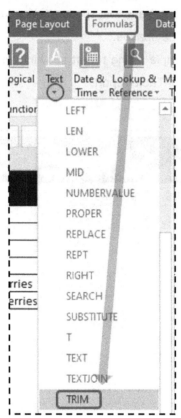

The Function Arguments dialogue box will appear:

4. Click cell '**A2**' or enter **A2** in the **Text** field
5. Click the '**OK**' button

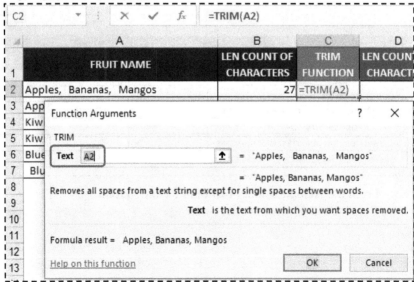

6. Select cell **'C2'** right-click and select **'Copy'** or press **Ctrl+C** on your keyboard

7. Select cells **'C3:C7'** and from your keyboard press shortcut keys **(CTRL+V)**

The extra spaces have been removed

	A	B LEN COUNT OF CHARACTERS	C TRIM FUNCTION	D LEN COUNT OF CHARACTERS
1	FRUIT NAME			
2	Apples, Bananas, Mangos	27	Apples, Bananas, Mangos	23
3	Apples, Bananas, Mangos	23	Apples, Bananas, Mangos	23
4	Kiwi, Oranges, Strawberries	27	Kiwi, Oranges, Strawberries	27
5	Kiwi, Oranges, Strawberries	29	Kiwi, Oranges, Strawberries	27
6	Blueberries, Raspberries, Blackberries	38	Blueberries, Raspberries, Blackberries	38
7	Blueberries, Raspberries, Blackberries	40	Blueberries, Raspberries, Blackberries	38

*Next, we'll copy and **paste as values** the contents of column C and remove the columns (B, C, D, & E) used for troubleshooting.*

8. Select cells **'C2:C7'**, click the **'Copy'** button or press **CTRL+C** from your keyboard

9. Select cell **'A2'**

10. **Right-click** and select **'Paste Special…'**

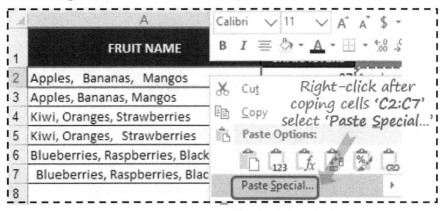

11. Select the **'Values'** radio button

12. Click the **'OK'** button

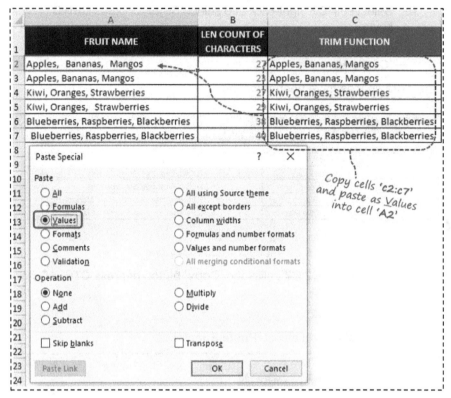

13. Select columns **'B', 'C', 'D', &'E'**

14. **Right-click** and select **'Delete'**, the troubleshooting columns **B'**, **'C',** **'D', & 'E'** should now be removed

We have successfully removed all extraneous spaces from the records contained in **column 'A'**. Further analysis and reporting may now be completed without error.

	A	B
1	**FRUIT NAME**	
2	Apples, Bananas, Mangos	
3	Apples, Bananas, Mangos	
4	Kiwi, Oranges, Strawberries	
5	Kiwi, Oranges, Strawberries	
6	Blueberries, Raspberries, Blackberries	
7	Blueberries, Raspberries, Blackberries	

CONCAT

Scenario:

You've been given a list of employees that need to be notified of a change in healthcare benefits. You've been asked to:

- Generate an email list based on these names

Sample data:

	A	B	C
1	FIRST NAME	LAST NAME	EMAIL ADDRESS
2	Billy	Winchester	
3	Helen	Smith	
4	Sally	Morton	
5	Jill	Johnson	
6	John	Dower	

1. Select the tab named **'CONCAT'**

2. Place your cursor in cell **'C2'**

3. From the Ribbon select **Formulas : Text: CONCAT**

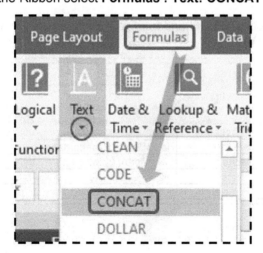

In the Function Arguments dialogue box enter the following:
- **Text1** box click cell '**A2**' or enter **A2**
- **Text2** box click cell '**B2**' or enter **B2**
- **Text3** box enter the text **@fakecompany.com**

4. Click the '**OK**' button

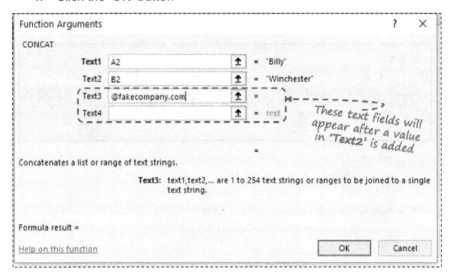

5. Select cell '**C2**' right-click and select '**Copy**' or press **Ctrl+C** on your keyboard

6. Select cells '**C3:C6**' and from your keyboard press shortcut keys (**CTRL+V**)

We now have an email list.

Alternatively, you may perform the same type of functionality WITHOUT using the formula wizard for CONCAT. Instead, by using the **ampersand**

(&) symbol. This is how many intermediate and advanced Excel® users typically execute this command. Please see below for an example:

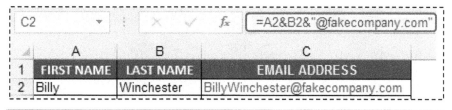

MID

Scenario

You've been given a list of stores from a database which prepends each location with three leading zeros. You need to add this store information into an existing spreadsheet that *does not have* the leading zeros for their store numbers. You plan on using the MID function to:

- Return the store number *without* the three leading zeros

Sample data:

	A	B
1	STORE NUMBER	STORE NUMBER (w/o leading zeros)
2	000111	
3	000222	
4	000333	
5	000444	
6	000555	

1. Select the tab named **'Mid'**

2. Place your cursor in cell **'B2'**

3. From the Ribbon select **Formulas : Text : MID**

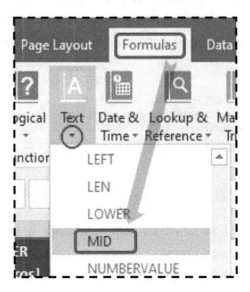

In the Function Arguments dialogue box enter the following:
- **Text** box click cell '**A2**' or enter **A2**
- **Start_num** enter the number **4** *(this is the position where the store number begins)*
- **Num_chars** enter the number **3** *(this is the number of characters to be returned, the 3 digit store number)*

4. Click the '**OK**' button

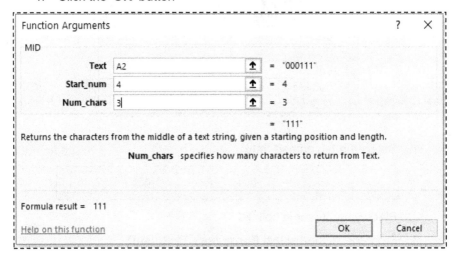

5. Select cell **'B2'** right-click and select **'Copy'** or press **Ctrl+C** on your keyboard

6. Select cells **'B3:B6'** and from your keyboard press shortcut keys **(CTRL+V)**

	A	B	B
1	STORE NUMBER	STORE NUMBER (w/o leading zeros)	STORE NUMBER (w/o leading zeros)
2	000111	111	=MID(A2,4,3)
3	000222	222	=MID(A3,4,3)
4	000333	333	=MID(A4,4,3)
5	000444	444	=MID(A5,4,3)
6	000555	555	=MID(A6,4,3)

We now have a list of store numbers without the three leading zeros.

CHAPTER 10

ROUNDING NUMBERS

FUNCTION	DEFINITION
ROUND	The ROUND function rounds a number to a specified number of digits.

Quick Examples:

```
ROUND - Syntax:
```
ROUND(number, **num_digits**)
All arguments are required

>   If **num_digits** is greater than 0 (zero), then the number is rounded
>   to the specified total of decimal places, otherwise the number is
>   rounded to the nearest integer

C5	▼	:	✕	✓	*fx*	=ROUND(A5,1)

	A	B	C	D
1	NUMBER	num_digits = 0	num_digits = 1	num_digits = 2
2	5	5	5	5
3	5.125	5	5.1	5.13
4	5.5	6	5.5	5.5
5	5.75	6	5.8	5.75

	A	B	C	D
1	NUMBER	num_digits = 0	num_digits = 1	num_digits = 2
2	5	=ROUND(A2,0)	=ROUND(A2,1)	=ROUND(A2,2)
3	5.125	=ROUND(A3,0)	=ROUND(A3,1)	=ROUND(A3,2)
4	5.5	=ROUND(A4,0)	=ROUND(A4,1)	=ROUND(A4,2)
5	5.75	=ROUND(A5,0)	=ROUND(A5,1)	=ROUND(A5,2)

WEB ADDRESS & FILE NAME FOR EXERCISE:
https://bentonbooks.wixsite.com/bentonbooks/excel-2019
Round.xlsx

Scenario:

You're a retail analyst and have been asked to report the average price of a list of products. After running a query against the sales database you realize the price per product extends four decimals and your customer prefers to see the price rounded to the nearest 10th, therefore, you need apply the ROUND function to the price to meet your customer's request.

Step-By-Step Example:

ROUND

Sample data:

	A	B	C
1	PRODUCT	AVERAGE PRICE	ROUNDED PRICE
2	Item_A	$1.7511	
3	Item_B	$2.3333	
4	Item_C	$3.6983	
5	Item_D	$4.3174	
6	Item_E	$5.8526	
7	Item_F	$6.4911	
8	Item_G	$8.8745	

1. Open the Round.xlsx spreadsheet
2. Place your cursor in cell **'C2'**
3. From the Ribbon select **Formulas : Math & Trig**
4. From the drop-down list, select the option **'ROUND'**

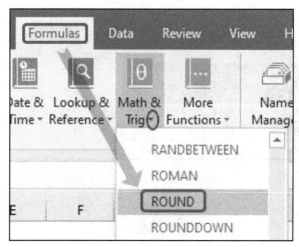

In the Function Arguments dialogue box enter the following:

- Click cell '**B2**' or enter **B2** in the dialogue box for the **'Number'** *(this is value we want to round)*

- For **'Num_digits'**, enter **1** *(this is the number of digits we want to round, the nearest 10th)*

5. Click the '**OK**' button

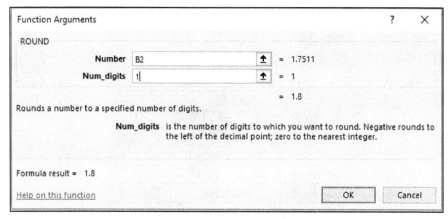

6. From the Ribbon select **Home** and **reduce the decimal by 2 places**, should be **$1.80**.

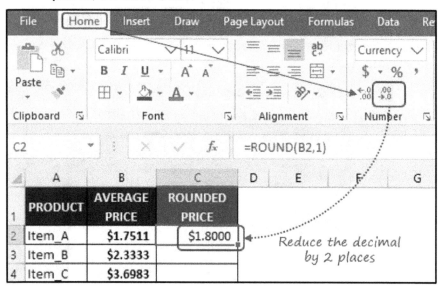

7. Select cell **'C2'** right-click and select **'Copy'** or press **Ctrl+C** on your keyboard

8. Select cells **'C3:C8'** and from your keyboard press shortcut keys **(CTRL+V)**

We now have an average price list rounded to the nearest 10th.

	A	B	C
	PRODUCT	AVERAGE PRICE	ROUNDED PRICE
1			
2	Item_A	$1.7511	$1.80
3	Item_B	$2.3333	$2.30
4	Item_C	$3.6983	$3.70
5	Item_D	$4.3174	$4.30
6	Item_E	$5.8526	$5.90
7	Item_F	$6.4911	$6.50
8	Item_G	$8.8745	$8.90

CHAPTER 11

VLOOKUP

FUNCTION	DEFINITION
VLOOKUP	The VLOOKUP function allows you to vertically search for a value from one Excel® list and return that specific value to a new Excel® list, based on a *matching lookup value*

Conceptual Example:

Need to add Employee Name to the Sales Report ⟶ Need to **lookup** Employee's Name based on their Sales ID

Employee Data

SALES PERSON ID	SALES PERSON NAME	REGION
800	Smith, Jack	East
200	Graham, Peter	West
1174	Steller, Alex	Central
500	Simpson, Helen	East
833	Tanner, Joe	West

SALES REPORT

SALES PERSON ID	Jan
200	$ 869
500	$ 1,975
800	$ 2,779
833	$ 7,716
1174	$ 5,620

Syntax Example:

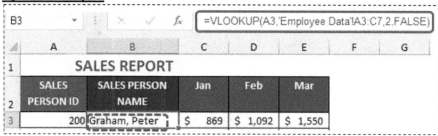

B3   fx   =VLOOKUP(A3,'Employee Data'!A3:C7,2,FALSE)

	A	B	C	D	E	F	G
1		SALES REPORT					
2	SALES PERSON ID	SALES PERSON NAME	Jan	Feb	Mar		
3	200	Graham, Peter	$ 869	$ 1,092	$ 1,550		

```
Syntax:
VLOOKUP (Lookup_value, Table_array, Col_index_num,
[Range_lookup])

All parameters are required, except for [Range_lookup]
```

THE 4 - PARTS OF A VLOOKUP (EXPLAINED)

❶ lookup value *(field to match)*:

The value you want to find (match) typically located in another worksheet or workbook.

    In the below example, cell **'A2'** on **'Sheet1'** is selected, which has the Sales Person ID value of **'200'**. We will look to match this value in the worksheet labeled **'Sheet2'**. *Sales Person Name* is the value we want to lookup and *be returned* to the tab labeled **'Sheet1'**.

❷ Table array *(where to search)*:

The spreadsheet and range of cells searched for the ❶ Lookup_value. The field you want to match *must be* in the *first column* of the range of cells you specify in the ❷ Table_array.

    In the below example, we're searching the tab labeled **'Sheet2'** with the cell range of **'A2:B6'**.

❸ Col index num *(what you want returned)*:

Is the column containing the value you want returned.

    In our example, column **'2'** of the tab labeled **'Sheet2'** contains the value of Sales Person Name which we want returned to the tab labeled **'Sheet1'**.

❹ Range lookup:

Is the optional value of **'TRUE'** or **'FALSE'**. The value of **'FALSE'** would return an *exact* match, while **'TRUE'** would return an approximate match.

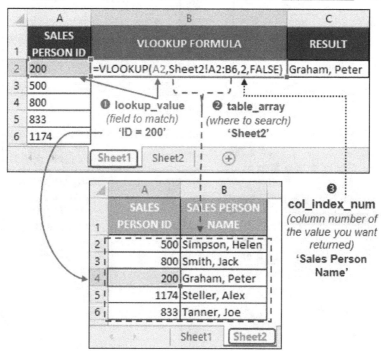

Step-By-Step Examples:

EXAMPLE 1: HOW-TO-APPLY A BASIC VLOOKUP FUNCTION

Scenario:

You've been asked to provide a list of first quarter sales by month for each sales person. You run a query from the sales database and generate an Excel® report. Unfortunately, the database only contains the sales person's ID, *but not their name*. You apply a VLOOKUP formula to return the Sales Person's Name from an existing Excel® spreadsheet to the new sales report.

WEB ADDRESS & FILE NAME FOR EXERCISE:
https://bentonbooks.wixsite.com/bentonbooks/excel-2019
Vlookup_Example_1.xlsx

Sample data:

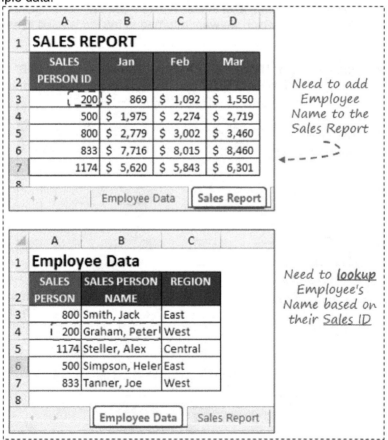

1. Open the Vlookup_Example_1.xlsx spreadsheet

2. Select the tab named **'Sales Report'**

3. Place your cursor in cell **'B3'**

4. From the Ribbon select **Formulas : Lookup & Reference**

5. From the drop-down list, select the option **'VLOOKUP'**

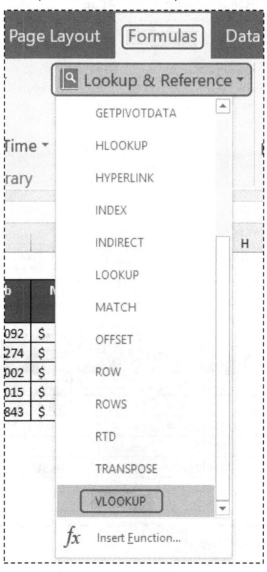

6. In the Function Arguments dialogue box enter the following:

   A. Click cell '**A3**' or enter **A3** in the dialogue box for the '**Lookup_value**' *(the sales person ID is the field we'll lookup on the 'Employee Data' tab)*

   B. For '**Table_array**', click on the tab '**Employee Data**' and select cells '**A3:C7**' *(this is the range of cells we're searching)*

   C. Enter the number **2** for '**Col_index_num**' *(this is the column number containing the sales person's name)*

   D. For '**Range_lookup**' enter **FALSE**

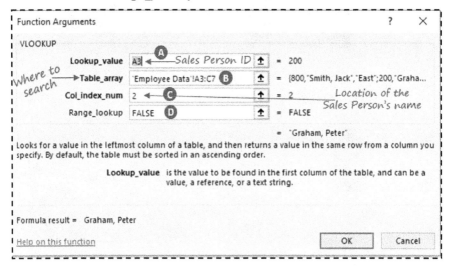

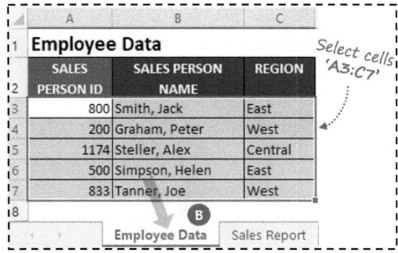

7. Click the '**OK**' button

The following result should now be displayed on the **Sales Report** worksheet:

| B3 | ▼ | : | × | ✓ | fx | =VLOOKUP(A3,'Employee Data'!A3:C7,2,FALSE) |

	A	B	C	D	E	F	G
1	**SALES REPORT**						
2	**SALES PERSON ID**	**SALES PERSON NAME**	**Jan**	**Feb**	**Mar**		
3	200	Graham, Peter	$ 869	$ 1,092	$ 1,550		
4	500		$ 1,975	$ 2,274	$ 2,719		
5	800		$ 2,779	$ 3,002	$ 3,460		
6	833		$ 7,716	$ 8,015	$ 8,460		
7	1174		$ 5,620	$ 5,843	$ 6,301		

8. We need to do one additional step before we can copy this formula down to cells '**B4:B7**'. We must add the U.S. dollar symbol **$** to the '**Table_array**'. This will prevent our cell range *(Table_array)* from changing:

↓↓ ↓↓

=VLOOKUP(A3,'Employee Data'!$A$3:$C$7,2,FALSE)

If we attempted to copy the VLOOKUP formula to cells '**B4:B7**' without adding the **$**, the result would be as follows, ***NOTE:*** *how the 'Table_array' cell range changes:*

	A	B
1	**SALES REPORT**	
2	**SALES PERSO**	**SALES PERSON NAME**
3	200	=VLOOKUP(A3,'Employee Data'!A3:C7,2,FALSE)
4	500	=VLOOKUP(A4,'Employee Data'!A4:C8,2,FALSE)
5	800	=VLOOKUP(A5,'Employee Data'!A5:C9,2,FALSE)
6	833	=VLOOKUP(A6,'Employee Data'!A6:C10,2,FALSE)
7	1174	=VLOOKUP(A7,'Employee Data'!A7:C11,2,FALSE)

Table_array changes

We would receive a **#N/A** error in cells '**B5**' & '**B7**'

⊿	A	B	C	D	E
1	**SALES REPORT**				
2	**SALES PERSON ID**	**SALES PERSON NAME**	**Jan**	**Feb**	**Mar**
3	200	Graham, Peter	$ 869	$ 1,092	$ 1,550
4	500	Simpson, Helen	$ 1,975	$ 2,274	$ 2,719
5	800	#N/A	$ 2,779	$ 3,002	$ 3,460
6	833	Tanner, Joe	$ 7,716	$ 8,015	$ 8,460
7	1174	#N/A	$ 5,620	$ 5,843	$ 6,301

9. Select cell **'B3'** after <u>updating</u> the formula to:
   `=VLOOKUP(A3,'Employee Data'!$A$3:$C$7,2,FALSE)`
   and right-click, select **'<u>C</u>opy'** or press **Ctrl+C** on your keyboard

10. Select cells **'B4:B7'** and from your keyboard press shortcut keys (**CTRL+V**)

⊿	A	B	C	D	E
1	**SALES REPORT**				
2	**SALES PERSON ID**	**SALES PERSON NAME**	**Jan**	**Feb**	**Mar**
3	200	Graham, Peter	$ 869	$ 1,092	$ 1,550
4	500	Simpson, Helen	$ 1,975	$ 2,274	$ 2,719
5	800	Smith, Jack	$ 2,779	$ 3,002	$ 3,460
6	833	Tanner, Joe	$ 7,716	$ 8,015	$ 8,460
7	1174	Steller, Alex	$ 5,620	$ 5,843	$ 6,301

⊿	A	B	C	D	E
1	**SALES REPORT**				
2	**SALES PERSON ID**	**SALES PERSON NAME**	**Jan**	**Feb**	**Mar**
3	200	=VLOOKUP(A3,'Employee Data'!$A$3:$C$7,2,FALSE)	869	1092	1550
4	500	=VLOOKUP(A4,'Employee Data'!$A$3:$C$7,2,FALSE)	1975	2274	2719
5	800	=VLOOKUP(A5,'Employee Data'!$A$3:$C$7,2,FALSE)	2779	3002	3460
6	833	=VLOOKUP(A6,'Employee Data'!$A$3:$C$7,2,FALSE)	7715.9	8014.9	8459.9
7	1174	=VLOOKUP(A7,'Employee Data'!$A$3:$C$7,2,FALSE)	5620	5843	6301

We have successfully looked-up and added the Sales Person Name to the quarterly sales report. We can now provide a list of the first quarter sales by month for each sales person.

Alternatively, for the **'Table_array'**, instead of entering the range of cells (Employee Data!$A$3:$C$7)and having to add the $ to hold the array constant, you may enter the entire column **A:C** (Employee Data !A:C), provided the *entire column* contains only the data you want returned. This would eliminate the need to complete **step 8**.

However, depending on the number of records you're looking up *(the size of your data)*, there could be a reduction in performance speed when selecting the entire column. Especially, when *combining* the VLOOKUP with other functions. Please see the below screenshots for a complete example using the entire column instead of a cell range:

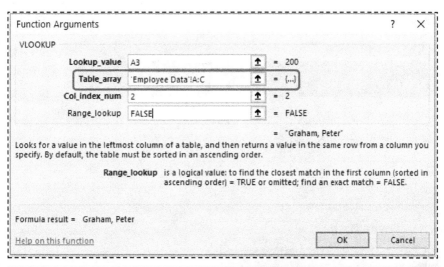

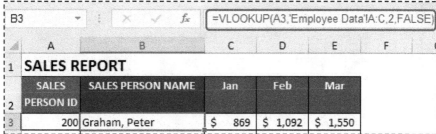

	A	B	C	D	E
1	SALES REPORT				
2	SALES PERSON ID	SALES PERSON NAME	Jan	Feb	Mar
3	200	=VLOOKUP(A3,'Employee Data'!A:C,2,FALSE)	869	1092	1550
4	500	=VLOOKUP(A4,'Employee Data'!A:C,2,FALSE)	1975	2274	2719
5	800	=VLOOKUP(A5,'Employee Data'!A:C,2,FALSE)	2779	3002	3460
6	833	=VLOOKUP(A6,'Employee Data'!A:C,2,FALSE)	7715.9	8014.9	8459.9
7	1174	=VLOOKUP(A7,'Employee Data'!A:C,2,FALSE)	5620	5843	6301

EXAMPLE 2: HOW-TO-APPLY A VLOOKUP USING THE ENTIRE COLUMN

Scenario:
You've now been asked to include the **sales region** to the list of first quarter sales by month, for each sales person.

WEB ADDRESS & FILE NAME FOR EXERCISE:
https://bentonbooks.wixsite.com/bentonbooks/excel-2019
Vlookup_Example_2.xlsx

Sample data:

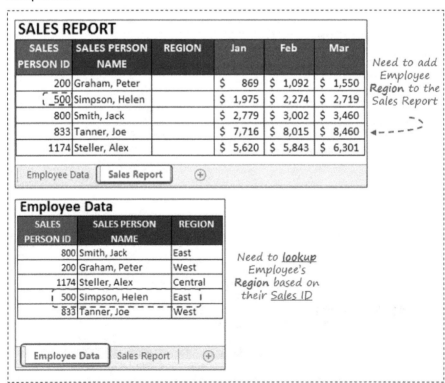

1. Open the Vlookup_Example_2.xlsx spreadsheet

2. Select the tab named **'Sales Report'**

3. Place your cursor in cell **'C3'**

4. From the Ribbon select **Formulas : Lookup & Reference**

5. From the drop-down list, select the option **'VLOOKUP'**

In the Function Arguments dialogue box enter the following:

- Click cell 'A3' or enter **A3** in the dialogue box for the **'Lookup_value'** *(the sales person ID is the field we'll lookup on the 'Employee Data' tab)*

- For **'Table_array'**, click on the tab **'Employee Data'** and select columns **'A:C'** *(this is the range of cells we're searching)*

- Enter the number **3** for **'Col_index_num'** *(this is the column containing the sales person's region)*

- For **'Range_lookup'** enter **FALSE**

6. Click the **'OK'** button

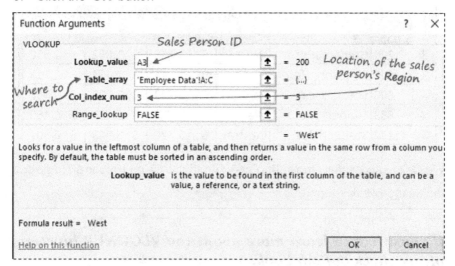

The following should be the result:

C3				f_x	=VLOOKUP(A3,'Employee Data'!A:C,3,FALSE)

	A	B	C	D	E	F
1	**SALES REPORT**					
2	SALES PERSON ID	SALES PERSON NAME	REGION	Jan	Feb	Mar
3	200	Graham, Peter	West	$ 869	$ 1,092	$ 1,550
4	500	Simpson, Helen		$ 1,975	$ 2,274	$ 2,719
5	800	Smith, Jack		$ 2,779	$ 3,002	$ 3,460
6	833	Tanner, Joe		$ 7,716	$ 8,015	$ 8,460
7	1174	Steller, Alex		$ 5,620	$ 5,843	$ 6,301

7. Select cell **'C3'** and right-click and select **'Copy'** or press **Ctrl+C** on your keyboard

8. Select cells **'C4:C7'** and from your keyboard press shortcut keys (**CTRL+V**)

The following should be the result:

	A	B	C	D	E	F
1	SALES PERS	SALES PERSON NAME	REGION	Jan	Feb	Mar
2	200	Graham, Peter	West	$ 869	$ 1,092	$ 1,550
3	500	Simpson, Helen	East	$ 1,975	$ 2,274	$ 2,719
4	800	Smith, Jack	East	$ 2,779	$ 3,002	$ 3,460
5	833	Tanner, Joe	West	$ 7,716	$ 8,015	$ 8,460
6	1174	Steller, Alex	Central	$ 5,620	$ 5,843	$ 6,301

We have successfully looked-up and added the Sales Person's **Region** to the quarterly sales report.

If you'd like to learn more about the VLOOKUP function, please check out our book:

Excel 2019 Vlookup The Step-By-Step Guide

https://bentonbooks.wixsite.com/bentonbooks/vlookup

CHAPTER 12

FUNCTION	DEFINITION
IF	IF formulas allow you test conditions and return one value *if true* and another *if false*
IFERROR	IFERROR <u>returns a value you specify</u> when the result of a function is an error such as: #N/A #VALUE! #REF! #DIV/0! #NUM! #NAME? #NULL! **Otherwise** IFERROR **will return the result** of the formula

Quick Examples:

```
IF - Syntax:
```
```
IF(logical_test, value_if_true, [value_if_false])
```
```
logic_test required, value_if_true required,
value_if_false optional
```

F2	▾	:	✕	✓	*fx*	=IF(B2=D2,"Pass","Fail")

	A	B	C	D	E	F
1	**RESULTS 1**	**COUNT**	**RESULTS 2**	**COUNT**		If results match, indicate with the word "Pass"
2	Test #1	111	Test #1	111		Pass
3	Test #2	161	Test #2	158		Fail

```
IFERROR Syntax:
```
```
IFERROR(value, value_if_error)
All parameters are required
```

121

E3			✕	✓	*fx*	=IFERROR(D3/C3,"No Orders")

◢	A	B	C	D	E	F	G
1	ITEM	COST	ORDERS	SALES TOTAL	AVG PRICE		
2	Bagels	$15	200	$3,500	$17.50		
3	Cookies	$9	0	$0	No Orders		

WEB ADDRESS & FILE NAME FOR EXERCISE:
https://bentonbooks.wixsite.com/bentonbooks/excel-2019
LogicExamples.xlsx

Step-By-Step Examples:

IF

Scenario:

You're a data analyst working on a project and need to compare test results:

- If the results match between the two datasets, insert the text **'Pass'**
- If the results DO NOT match, insert the text **'Fail'**

Sample data:

◢	A	B	C	D	E	F
1	RESULTS A	COUNT	RESULTS B	COUNT		IF the results match, indicate with the text "Pass", otherwise use the text "Fail"
2	Test #1	111	Test #1	111		
3	Test #2	161	Test #2	158		
4	Test #3	183	Test #3	175		
5	Test #4	243	Test #4	243		
6	Test #5	263	Test #5	260		

1. Open the LogicExamples.xlsx spreadsheet

2. Select the tab named **'IF'**

3. Place your cursor in cell **'F2'**

4. From the Ribbon select **Formulas : Logical**

5. From the drop-down list, select the option **'IF'**

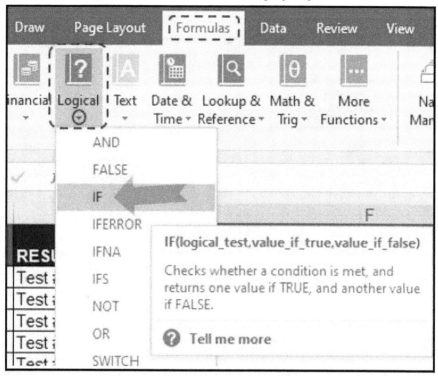

6. In the Function Arguments dialogue box enter the following:
   Logical_test   B2=D2
   Value_if_true "Pass"
   Value_if_false "Fail"

7. Click the '**OK**' button

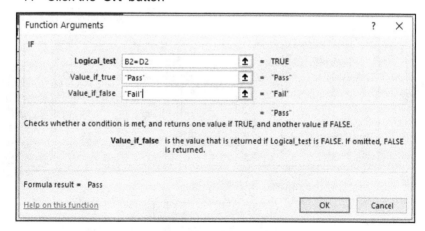

8. Select cell **'F2'** right-click and select **'Copy'** or press **Ctrl+C** on your keyboard

9. Select cells **'F3:F6'** and from your keyboard press shortcut keys (**CTRL+V**)

The results should be as follows:

F2		✗	✓	fx	=IF(B2=D2,"Pass","Fail")

	A	B	C	D	E	F
						IF the results match, indicate with the text
1	RESULTS A	COUNT	RESULTS B	COUNT		"Pass", otherwise use the text "Fail"
2	Test #1	111	Test #1	111		Pass
3	Test #2	161	Test #2	158		Fail
4	Test #3	183	Test #3	175		Fail
5	Test #4	243	Test #4	243		Pass
6	Test #5	263	Test #5	260		Fail

We've now compared two datasets and indicated if the results passed or failed.

IFERROR

Scenario:

A manager has asked you to *"fix"* a spreadsheet as they do not want to see the error message **#DIV/0!** for the average price calculations when there are zero orders. Instead, they would like the report to display the text "**No Orders**."

Sample data:

	A	B	C	D	E
1	ITEM	COST	ORDERS	SALES TOTAL	AVG PRICE
2	Bagels	$15	200	$3,500	$17.50
3	Cookies	$9	0	$0	#DIV/0!
4	Cup Cakes	$24	175	$4,725	$27.00
5	Donuts	$12	200	$2,370	$11.85
6	Pastries	$8	0	$0	#DIV/0!

1. Select the tab named **'IFERROR'**

2. Place your cursor in cell **'E2'** and **DELETE** the existing formula

3. From the Ribbon select **Formulas : Logical**

4. From the drop-down list, select the option **'IFERROR'**

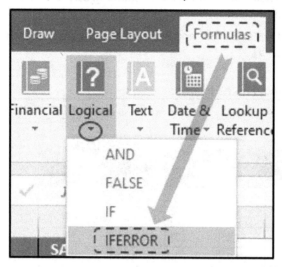

5. In the Function Arguments dialogue box enter the following:
   Value   D2/C2
   Value_if_error   No Orders

6. Click the '**OK**' button

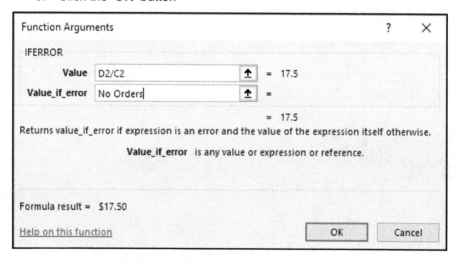

7. Select cell **'E2'** right-click and select **'Copy'** or press **Ctrl+C** on your keyboard

8. Select cells **'E3:E6'** and from your keyboard press shortcut keys **(CTRL+V)**

The results should be as follows:

| E3 | | | | | f_x | =IFERROR(D3/C3,"No Orders") |

▲	A	B	C	D	E	F	G
1	ITEM	COST	ORDERS	SALES TOTAL	AVG PRICE		
2	Bagels	$15	200	$3,500	$17.50		
3	Cookies	$9	0	$0	No Orders		
4	Cup Cakes	$24	175	$4,725	$27.00		
5	Donuts	$12	200	$2,370	$11.85		
6	Pastries	$8	0	$0	No Orders		

We've now fixed the average price display text when there are zero orders to be "No Orders," instead of the error message **#DIV/0!**

CHAPTER 13

CONDITIONAL FUNCTIONS

FUNCTION	DEFINITION
SumIF	SumIF sums the values in a range based on the criteria you identify
AverageIF	AverageIF returns the average value (number) in a range of cells based on the criteria you identify
CountIF	CountIF counts the number of times a value appears in a range of cells based on the criteria you identify
CountIFS	CountIFS counts the number of times a value appears in a range of cells based on the criteria you identify, *across multiple ranges*

Syntax:

SumIF:

SUMIF(range, criteria, [sum_range])

range and **criteria** are required, **sum_range** is optional

AverageIF:

AVERAGEIF(range, criteria, [average_range])

range and **criteria** are required, **average_range** is optional

CountIF:

COUNTIF(range, criteria)

range and **criteria** are required

CountIFS:

COUNTIFS(criteria_range1, criteria1, [criteria_range2, criteria2]…)

criteria_range1 and **criteria1** are required, additional **criteria ranges** and **criteria** are optional

Quick Examples:

	A	B	C	D	E	F	G	H	I
1	REGION	QTR	APPLES SALES		QTR	SumIF FORMULA	RESULT	AverageIF FORMULA	RESULT
2	Central	1	235		Q1	=SUMIF(B:B,1,C:C)	884	=AVERAGEIF(B:B,1,C:C)	295
3	Central	2	285		Q2	=SUMIF(B:B,2,C:C)	1034	=AVERAGEIF(B:B,2,C:C)	344
4	Central	3	307		Q3	=SUMIF(B:B,3,C:C)	1166	=AVERAGEIF(B:B,3,C:C)	388
5	Central	4	367		Q4	=SUMIF(B:B,4,C:C)	1346	=AVERAGEIF(B:B,4,C:C)	449
6	East	1	272						
7	East	2	322			*What are the total sales by QTR?*		*What are the average sales by QTR?*	
8	East	3	410						
9	East	4	470						
10	West	1	377						
11	West	2	427						
12	West	3	449						
13	West	4	509						

	A	B	C	D	E	J	K	L	M
1	REGION	QTR	APPLES SALES		QTR	CountIFS FORMULA	RESULT	CountIF FORMULA	RESULT
2	Central	1	235		Q1	=COUNTIFS(B:B,1,C:C,">400")	0	=COUNTIF(C:C,">400")	5
3	Central	2	285		Q2	=COUNTIFS(B:B,2,C:C,">400")	1		
4	Central	3	307		Q3	=COUNTIFS(B:B,3,C:C,">400")	2		
5	Central	4	367		Q4	=COUNTIFS(B:B,4,C:C,">400")	2		
6	East	1	272					*How many times for all QTRs were sales greater than 400?*	
7	East	2	322						
8	East	3	410			*How many times per QTR were sales greater than 400?*			
9	East	4	470						
10	West	1	377						
11	West	2	427						
12	West	3	449						
13	West	4	509						

WEB ADDRESS & FILE NAME FOR EXERCISE:

https://bentonbooks.wixsite.com/bentonbooks/excel-2019
Conditional_Functions.xlsx

Step-By-Step Examples:

Sample Data

	A	B	C
1	REGION	QUARTER	APPLES SALES
2	Central	1	$ 235
3	Central	2	$ 285
4	Central	3	$ 307
5	Central	4	$ 367
6	East	1	$ 272
7	East	2	$ 322
8	East	3	$ 410
9	East	4	$ 470
10	West	1	$ 377
11	West	2	$ 427
12	West	3	$ 449
13	West	4	$ 509

Scenario:

You've been given a spreadsheet that contains the Apple sales by quarter for three regions. You've been asked to summarize the data and provide the following information:

- What are the **total** sales by quarter?
- What are the **average** sales by quarter?
- **How many times** _per quarter_ were sales greater than $400?
- **Total number of times** for _all_ quarters, sales were greater than $400?

Step-By-Step Examples:

SUMIF

What are the **total** sales by quarter?

1. Open the spreadsheet Conditional_Functions.xlsx
2. Place your cursor in cell **'F2'**
3. From the Ribbon select the tab '**Formulas**'
4. Click fx **Insert Function**

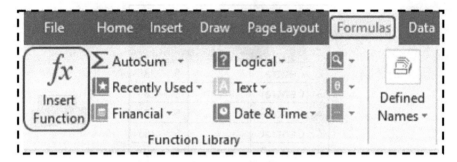

The following dialogue box will appear:

5. Type '**SumIF**' in the '**Search for a function:**' box
6. Click the '**Go**' button

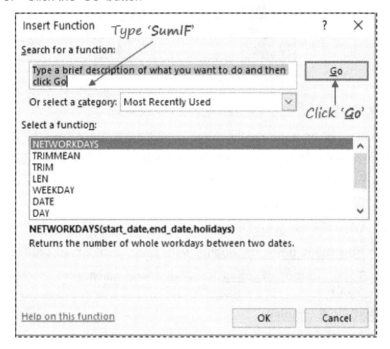

7. When prompted, select **'SUMIF'**:

8. Click the **'OK'** button

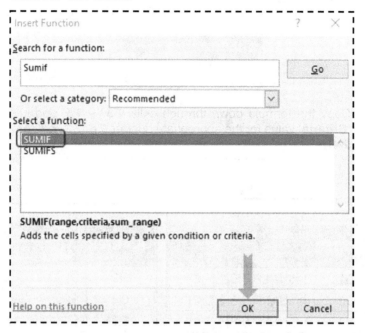

In the Function Arguments dialogue box enter the following:

    A. For the **Range** click the **column 'B'** *(this column lists the quarter)*

    B. For the **Criteria** enter **'1'** for Quarter 1 *(note: if this were a text field, you would encapsulate the text with double quotes " ")*

    C. For the **Sum_range** click the **column 'C'** *(this column lists the Apple sales)*

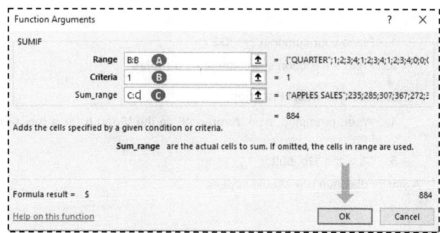

9. Click the '**OK**' button

The result for Q1 sales is **$884**:

E	F
QUARTER	SumIF Sales By QTR
Q1	$ 884

10. Copy the formula down through cells '**F3**' – '**F5**' and change the '**Criteria**' value for the appropriate quarter (*i.e. **2,3, & 4 for quarters 2-4***)

Quarter change

E	F
QUARTER	SumIF Sales By QTR
Q1	=SUMIF(B:B,1,C:C)
Q2	=SUMIF(B:B,2,C:C)
Q3	=SUMIF(B:B,3,C:C)
Q4	=SUMIF(B:B,4,C:C)

Results

E	F
QUARTER	SumIF Sales By QTR
Q1	$ 884
Q2	$ 1,034
Q3	$ 1,166
Q4	$ 1,346

*Change the quarter number (**Criteria**)*

AVERAGEIF

- What are the **average** sales by quarter?

1. Place your cursor in cell '**G2**'

2. From the Ribbon select the tab '**Formulas**'

3. Click *fx* **Insert Function**

4. When prompted, type '**AverageIF**' in the '**Search for a function:**' box

5. Click the '**Go**' button

A *similar* dialogue box should appear:

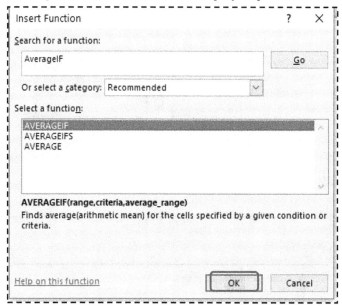

6. Click the '**OK**' button:

In the Function Arguments dialogue box enter the following:

    A. For the **Range** click the **column 'B'** *(this column lists the quarter)*

    B. For the **Criteria** enter **'1'** for Quarter 1 *(note: if this were a text field, you would encapsulate the text with double quotes " ")*

    C. For the **Average_range** click the **column 'C'** *(this column lists the Apple sales)*

7. Click the '**OK**' button

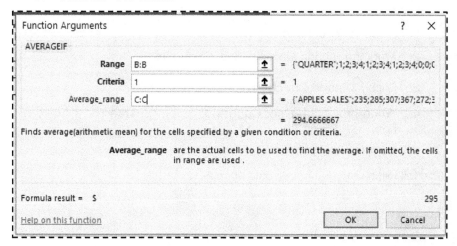

The **average sales** for Q1 are **$295:**

E	F	G
QUARTER	**SumIF** Sales By QTR	**AverageIF** Avg. Sales By QTR
Q1	$ 884	$ 295

8. Copy the formula down through cells **'G3' – 'G5'** and change the **'Criteria'** value for the appropriate quarter *(i.e. **2,3, & 4 for quarters 2-4)***

Quarter change

E	G
QUARTER	**AverageIF** Avg. Sales By QTR
Q1	=AVERAGEIF(B:B,1,C:C)
Q2	=AVERAGEIF(B:B,2,C:C)
Q3	=AVERAGEIF(B:B,3,C:C)
Q4	=AVERAGEIF(B:B,4,C:C)

Change the quarter number (Criteria)

Results

E	G
QUARTER	**AverageIF** Avg. Sales By QTR
Q1	$ 295
Q2	$ 345
Q3	$ 389
Q4	$ 449

COUNTIFS

- **How many times** per quarter were sales greater than $400?

In this example, we need to determine two items: A) the quarter **_AND_** B) the number of times sales were greater than $400

1. Place your cursor in cell **'H2'**

2. From the Ribbon select the tab '**Formulas'**

3. Click *fx* **Insert Function**

4. When prompted, type '**CountIFS'** in the '**Search for a function:'** box

5. Click the '**Go'** button

The following dialogue box should appear:

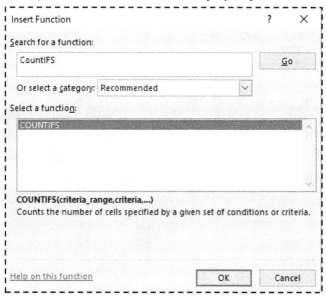

6. Click the '**OK**' button:

In the Function Arguments dialogue box enter the following:

    A. For the **Criteria_range1** click **column 'B'**

    B. For the **Criteria1** enter **'1'** for Quarter 1

    C. For the **Criteria_range2** click **column 'C'**

    D. For the **Criteria2** enter **">400"** for sales greater than $400, *(make sure >400 is in double quotes " ")*

7. Click the '**OK**' button

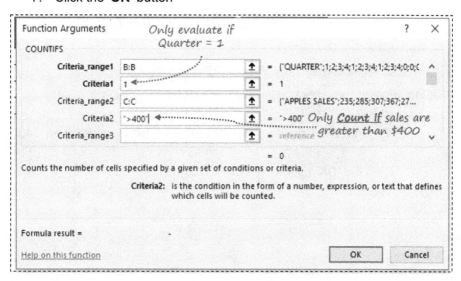

8. Copy the formula down through cells **'H3'** – **'H5'** and change the **'Criteria1'** value for the appropriate quarter *(i.e. **2,3, & 4 for quarters 2-4**)*

			Quarter change		Results	
A	B	C	E	H	E	H
REGION	QTR	APPLES SALES	QTR	CountIFS Sales By QTR >$400	QUARTER	CountIFS Sales By QTR >$400
2 Central	1	235	Q1	=COUNTIFS(B:B,1,C:C,">400")	Q1	–
3 Central	2	285	Q2	=COUNTIFS(B:B,2,C:C,">400")	Q2	1
4 Central	3	307	Q3	=COUNTIFS(B:B,3,C:C,">400")	Q3	2
5 Central	4	367	Q4	=COUNTIFS(B:B,4,C:C,">400")	Q4	2
6 East	1	272				
7 East	2	322				
8 East	3	410		*Change the quarter*		*Results equal to 0*
9 East	4	470		*number (**Criteria**)*		*(zero) are displayed*
10 West	1	377				*as a – (dash)*
11 West	2	427				
12 West	3	449				
13 West	4	509				

COUNTIF

- The **total number of times** over *all* quarters, sales were greater than $400?

1. Place your cursor in cell **'J2'**

2. From the Ribbon select the tab '**Formulas**'

3. Click *fx* **Insert Function**

4. When prompted, type '**CountIF**' in the '**Search for a function:**' box

5. Click the '**Go**' button

6. Select '**CountIF**' and click the '**OK**' button:

In the Function Arguments dialogue box enter the following:

    A. For the **Range** click the **column 'C'**

    B. For the **Criteria** enter **">400"** for sales greater than $400, *(make sure >400 is in double quotes " ")*

7. Click the '**OK**' button

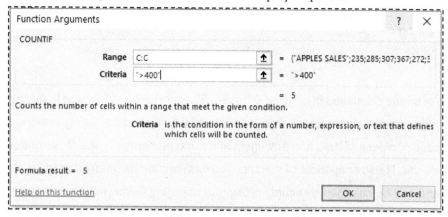

The result is; **5 times** over all quarters, sales were greater than $400

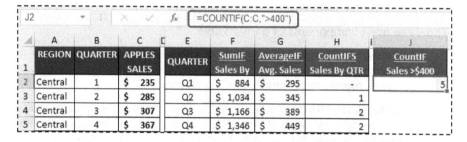

To see a completed example of this chapter, please select the worksheet:
'Completed Example' of the Conditional_Functions.xlsx workbook.

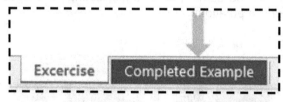

CHAPTER 14

As briefly discussed in chapter 3 (page 35), PivotTables allow you to quickly organize and summarize large amounts of information by taking individual cells or pieces of data and arranging them into numerous types of calculated views. These snapshots of summarized data require minimal effort to create and can be changed by simply clicking or dragging fields within your report.

Let's now take a closer look and walk through an example on how to create a basic PivotTable.

WHAT ARE THE MAIN PARTS OF A PIVOTTABLE?

The three main components of a PivotTable:

1. **Rows:** The rows section typically represents how you would like to categorize or group your data. Some examples include: employee name, region, department, part number etc.

2. **Columns:** The columns show the level or levels in which you're displaying your calculations. Often a *time period* such as a month, quarter, or year, but can also be categories, product lines, etc.

3. **Values:** Values are the calculation portion of the report, these figures can be sums, percentages, counts, averages, rankings or custom computations.

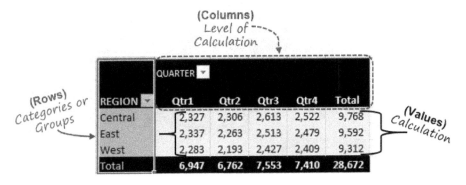

Next, we will review the fundamental steps of creating and modifying a Pivot Table. Here we will take a basic spreadsheet containing fruit sale information and:

- Determine the total fruit sales by region *and* quarter

WEB ADDRESS & FILE NAME FOR EXERCISE:
https://bentonbooks.wixsite.com/bentonbooks/excel-2019
FruitSales.xlsx

STEP-BY-STEP EXAMPLE: HOW TO CREATE A BASIC PIVOTTABLE

Sample data, due to space limitations **the entire data set is not displayed**.

	A	B	C	D	E	F	G	H	I
1	REGION	SALES PERSON FIRST NAME	SALES PERSON LAST NAME	SALES PERSON ID	QUARTER	APPLES	ORANGES	MANGOS	TOTAL
2	Central	Bob	Taylor	1174	1	1,810	2,039	1,771	5,620
3	Central	Helen	Smith	833	1	102	354	59	516
4	Central	Jill	Johnson	200	1	93	322	54	469
5	Central	Sally	Morton	500	1	595	824	556	1,975
6	Central	Sam	Becker	800	1	863	1,092	824	2,779
7	East	Abbey	Williams	690	1	346	237	260	843
8	East	John	Dower	255	1	260	178	195	633
9	East	John	Wilson	300	1	286	196	215	696
10	East	Mary	Nelson	600	1	315	215	236	766
11	East	Sarah	Taylor	900	1	381	261	285	927
12	West	Alex	Steller	1000	1	163	212	127	502
13	West	Billy	Winchester	1156	1	179	234	140	552
14	West	Helen	Simpson	817	1	148	193	116	457
15	West	Jack	Smith	100	1	111	145	87	343
16	West	Joe	Tanner	400	1	122	160	96	377
17	West	Peter	Graham	700	1	134	175	105	415
18	Central	Bob	Taylor	1174	2	113	390	65	567
19	Central	Helen	Smith	833	2	1,006	1,393	940	3,338
64	West	Joe	Tanner	400	4	2,833	2,886	2,796	8,516
65	West	Peter	Graham	700	4	4,392	4,473	4,334	13,199

1. Open the FruitSales.xlsx spreadsheet and select **cells 'A1:I65'**

2. From the Ribbon select **Insert : PivotTable**

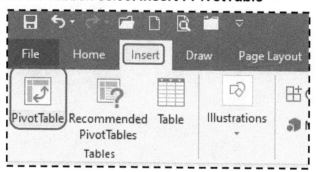

The following dialogue box will **appear**, please note the **Data Range** and **location where the new PivotTable will be located**:

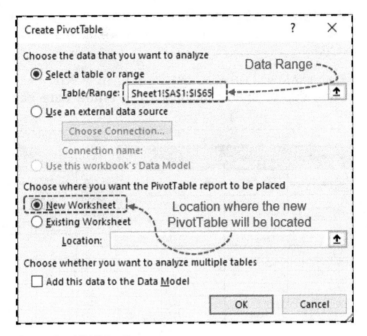

3. Click the '**OK**' button

A new tab will be created and appear similar to the following. *Note: the 'PivotTable Fields' pane on the right side of the new worksheet.*

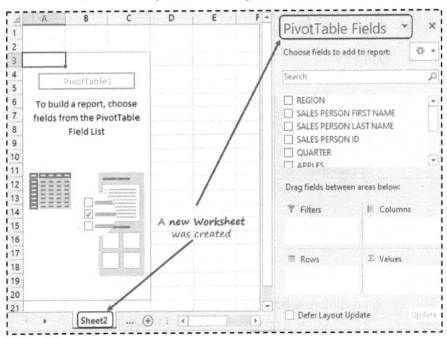

Next, we'll **categorize** our report and select a **calculation** value.

4. In the **'*PivotTable Fields' pane*** select the following fields:
   - **REGION** *(Rows section)*
   - **TOTAL** *(∑ Values section)*

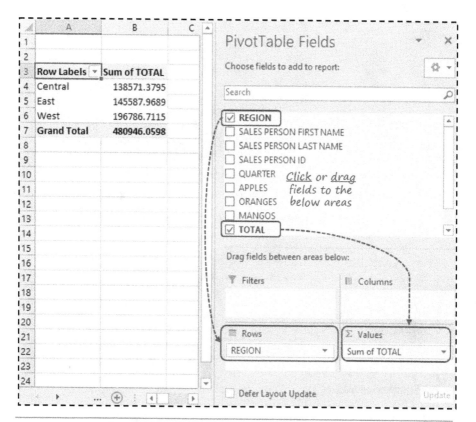

WHY DO THE '∑ VALUES' FIELDS SOMETIMES DEFAULT TO *COUNT* INSTEAD OF *SUM*?

When PivotTable source data contains blank rows, for example when selecting the entire column such as (Sheet1!$A:$I) instead of a specific cell rage (Sheet1!$A$1:$I$65), Excel® will default the calculation of a field added to the '∑ **Values**' section to **count** instead of **sum**.

If this happens, to change the '∑ **Values**' section from **count** to **sum**:

- Click the **'Count of TOTAL'** drop-down arrow, then from the sub-menu select **'Value Field Settings…'**

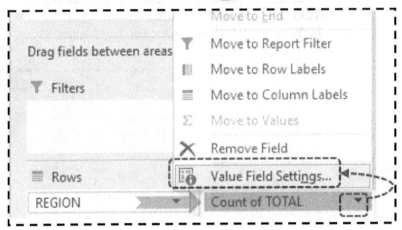

The following **'Value Field Settings…'** dialogue box will appear:

- From the **'Summarize value field by'** list, select the **'Sum'** option

- Click the **'OK'** button

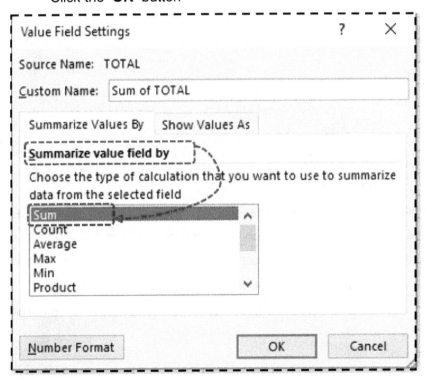

Continuing with our example:

The following should be displayed on the left side of your screen.
Note: the format is not very easy to read.

	A	B
1		
2		
3	Row Labels ▾	Sum of TOTAL
4	Central	138571.3795
5	East	145587.9689
6	West	196786.7115
7	Grand Total	480946.0598

5. We can change the column labels and format of the numbers. In the below example:

- Select cell '**A3**' and change the text from '**Row Labels**' to '**REGION**'

- Select cell '**B3**' and change the text from '**Sum of TOTAL**' to '**TOTAL SALES**'

- You may also change the currency format in cells '**B4:B7**'. In the below example, the format was changed to U.S. dollars with *zero* decimal places

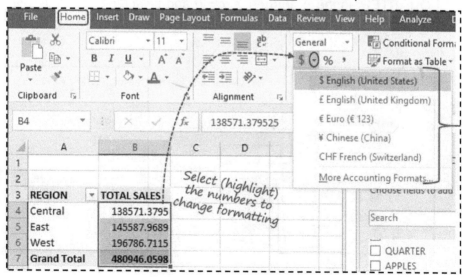

Below is the formatted example:

◢	A	B
1		
2		
3	**REGION** ▾	**TOTAL SALES**
4	Central	$ 138,571
5	East	$ 145,588
6	West	$ 196,787
7	**Grand Total**	$ **480,946**

To enhance the report further we're going to add *Quarter columns*.

This "level" dimension will provide greater detail of the total fruit sales.

6. Inside the *'PivotTable Fields' pane* **drag** the **'QUARTER'** field to the **'Columns'** section.

IMPORTANT!
Excel® is reading the **'Quarter'** as a numeric value, therefore if you click, **instead of drag** the field to the 'Columns' section, Excel® will apply a calculation.
If this happens, click the drop-down arrow for **'Sum of QUARTER'** in the **'Σ Values'** section and select the option **'Move to Column Labels'**

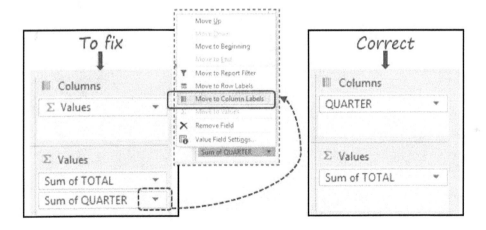

We now have **'QUARTER'** added to the summary

7. Select cell **'B3'** and change the text from **'Column Labels'** to **'BY QUARTER'**

8. The labels for cells **'B4'**, **'C4'**, **'D4'**, & **'E4'** were changed by adding the abbreviation text **'QTR'** in front of each quarter number

Before *formatting:*

◢	A	B	C	D	E	F
1						
2						
3	TOTAL SALES	Column Labels ▾				
4	REGION ▾	1	2	3		4 Grand Total
5	Central	$ 11,359	$ 19,352	$ 34,097	$ 73,763	$ 138,571
6	East	$ 3,865	$ 19,343	$ 38,811	$ 83,569	$ 145,588
7	West	$ 2,646	$ 23,586	$ 42,590	$ 127,964	$ 196,787
8	Grand Total	$ 17,870	$ 62,281	$ 115,499	$ 285,296	$ 480,946

After *formatting:*

TOTAL SALES	BY QUARTER ▾				
REGION ▾	QTR 1	QTR 2	QTR 3	QTR 4	Grand Total
Central	$ 11,359	$ 19,352	$ 34,097	$ 73,763	$ 138,571
East	$ 3,865	$ 19,343	$ 38,811	$ 83,569	$ 145,588
West	$ 2,646	$ 23,586	$ 42,590	$ 127,964	$ 196,787
Grand Total	$ 17,870	$ 62,281	$ 115,499	$ 285,296	$ 480,946

HOW TO DRILL-DOWN PIVOTTABLE DATA

Let's say you wanted to investigate further why the *Central Region's Q1 results* are so much higher than the East & West regions.

TOTAL SALES	BY QUARTER ▾
REGION ▾	QTR 1
Central	$ 11,359
East	$ 3,865
West	$ 2,646
Grand Total	$ 17,870

PivotTables allow you to **double-click on any calculated value to see the detail of that cell**. By double clicking the value, this will create a *new worksheet* containing an Excel® *table* with the details of that cell.

- For example, double-click on the calculated value in cell **'B5'**

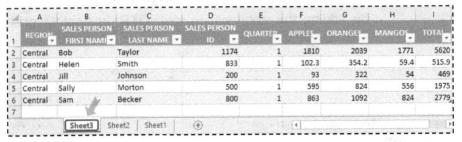

	A	B	C	D	E	F	G	H	I
1	REGION	SALES PERSON FIRST NAME	SALES PERSON LAST NAME	SALES PERSON ID	QUARTER	APPLES	ORANGES	MANGOS	TOTAL
2	Central	Bob	Taylor	1174	1	1810	2039	1771	5620
3	Central	Helen	Smith	833	1	102.3	354.2	59.4	515.9
4	Central	Jill	Johnson	200	1	93	322	54	469
5	Central	Sally	Morton	500	1	595	824	556	1975
6	Central	Sam	Becker	800	1	863	1092	824	2779
7									

Sheet3 | Sheet2 | Sheet1

- To delete the table (Sheet3), **right-click** on **'Sheet3'** and select **'Delete'**

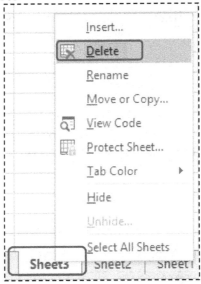

Insert...

Delete

Rename

Move or Copy...

View Code

Protect Sheet...

Tab Color ▶

Hide

Unhide...

Select All Sheets

Sheet3 | Sheet2 | Sheet1

- You'll receive the following message, click the **'Delete'** button

Microsoft Excel ✕

⚠ Microsoft Excel will permanently delete this sheet. Do you want to continue?

Delete   Cancel

These are just few examples of the powerful PivotTable functionality, *if you'd like to learn more, please check out our book:*

Excel 2019 Pivot Tables & Introduction To Dashboards The Step-By-Step Guide

https://bentonbooks.wixsite.com/bentonbooks/pivot-tables

With this practical and to-the-point guide you'll develop extensive skills to build and modify reports including how to:
- Organize and summarize large amounts of data
- Format & filter Pivot Table results
- Create Pivot Charts
- Display averages & percentages
- Group data into predefined ranges
- Use **Slicers, Timelines**, and **Sparklines**
- Rank results
- Apply calculated fields
- Use **Power Query** to create and combine Pivot Table reports from imported files
- And more!

Dashboards:
In addition to the above, you will also learn how **to create, format**, and **update** a **basic Dashboard** using PivotTable data:
- Incorporate **Pivot Charts, Sparklines**, and **performance symbols** into your reporting
- **Refresh** and **protect** your PivotTable data

A great resource for:
- Business Analysts
- Data Analysts
- Financial Analysts
- Administrative and Support staff

CHAPTER 15

The following lists some of the most common Microsoft® Excel® shortcuts:

DESCRIPTION	COMMANDS
FORMATTING	
CTRL+B	Applies or removes **bold** formatting
CTRL+I	Applies or removes *italic* formatting
CTRL+U	Applies or removes underlining formatting
FUNCTION	
CTRL+A	Selects (highlights) the entire worksheet
CTRL+C	Copies the contents of selected (highlighted) cells
CTRL+X	Cuts the selected cells
CTRL+V	Pastes the contents of selected (highlighted) cells, including cell formatting
CTRL+F	Displays the Find and Replace dialog box, with the **Find** tab selected
CTRL+H	Displays the Find and Replace dialog box, with the **Replace** tab selected
CTRL+K	Displays the Insert Hyperlink dialog box for new hyperlinks or the Edit Hyperlink dialog box for selected existing hyperlinks
CTRL+N	Creates a new blank workbook
CTRL+O	Displays the dialog box to open a file
CTRL+S	Saves the active file with its current file name, location, and file format
CTRL+P	Displays the Print dialog box
CTRL+Z	The undo function will reverse the last command or to delete the last entry you typed
ESC	Cancels an entry in the active cell or 'Formula Bar'

Shortcuts continued:

NAVIGATION	
CTRL+PageUp	Switches between worksheet tabs, from **right-to-left**
CTRL+PageDown	Switches between worksheet tabs, from **left-to-right**
CTRL+↓	Goes to the last row with content for the active column
CTRL+↑	Goes to the first row with content for the active column
CTRL+→	Goes to the last column with content for the active row
CTRL+Home	Goes to cell A1 of the active worksheet
Shift + F3	Opens the Excel formula window
EDITING	
F7	Runs Spellcheck
Shift + F7	Opens the thesaurus dialogue box

Thank you!

Your opinion?

Thank you for purchasing and reading this book, we hope you found it helpful! Your feedback is valued and appreciated! Please take a few minutes and leave a review.

QUESTIONS / FEEDBACK

Email: bentontrainingbooks@gmail.com
Website: https://bentonbooks.wixsite.com/bentonbooks